HOW TO USE THIS BOOK

When you're reading the book look out for 'animal sighting … these will show you the best places for nature-watching all over ea… SMALL LABELS indicate buildings. **LARGE LABELS** indicate areas. *ITALICS* indicate parks, lakes and seas.

AFRICA

ASIA

OCEANIA

THE CITY

Our cities are an urban jungle of tall apartment blocks, bright street lights, hurtling traffic, shops, houses and parks. The largest are home to millions of people – but a growing number of animals are living in our cities, too.

Some animals have lived alongside people for centuries, but others have been forced to adapt because their habitats are shrinking in the face of growing towns and cities. As urban areas continue to expand, we're sure to see more and more wildlife on our doorsteps. Not all species will cope with the speed of the change, but our efforts can help protect their futures. From wildlife reserves to squirrel highways, conservation programmes around the world are already ensuring there's a safe place for animals in our cities – and this book shows some of the ways that humans and animals are living side-by-side.

Here you can explore 38 city maps across six different continents and discover the incredible wildlife living there. While you wander the streets you'll encounter everything from widely spotted species to rare and sometimes surprising sightings. So turn the page to start your round-the-world adventure, and see what urban wonders await you...

NORTH AMERICA

North America has many landscapes, from the sweeping plains of the Midwest to towering mountain ranges to hot, rocky deserts. Its biggest cities are mostly along the Atlantic and Pacific coasts, and the region's wildlife often strays into these urban habitats. Some, like raccoons, are everyday visitors while others, such as shy black bears, make for incredible animal stories!

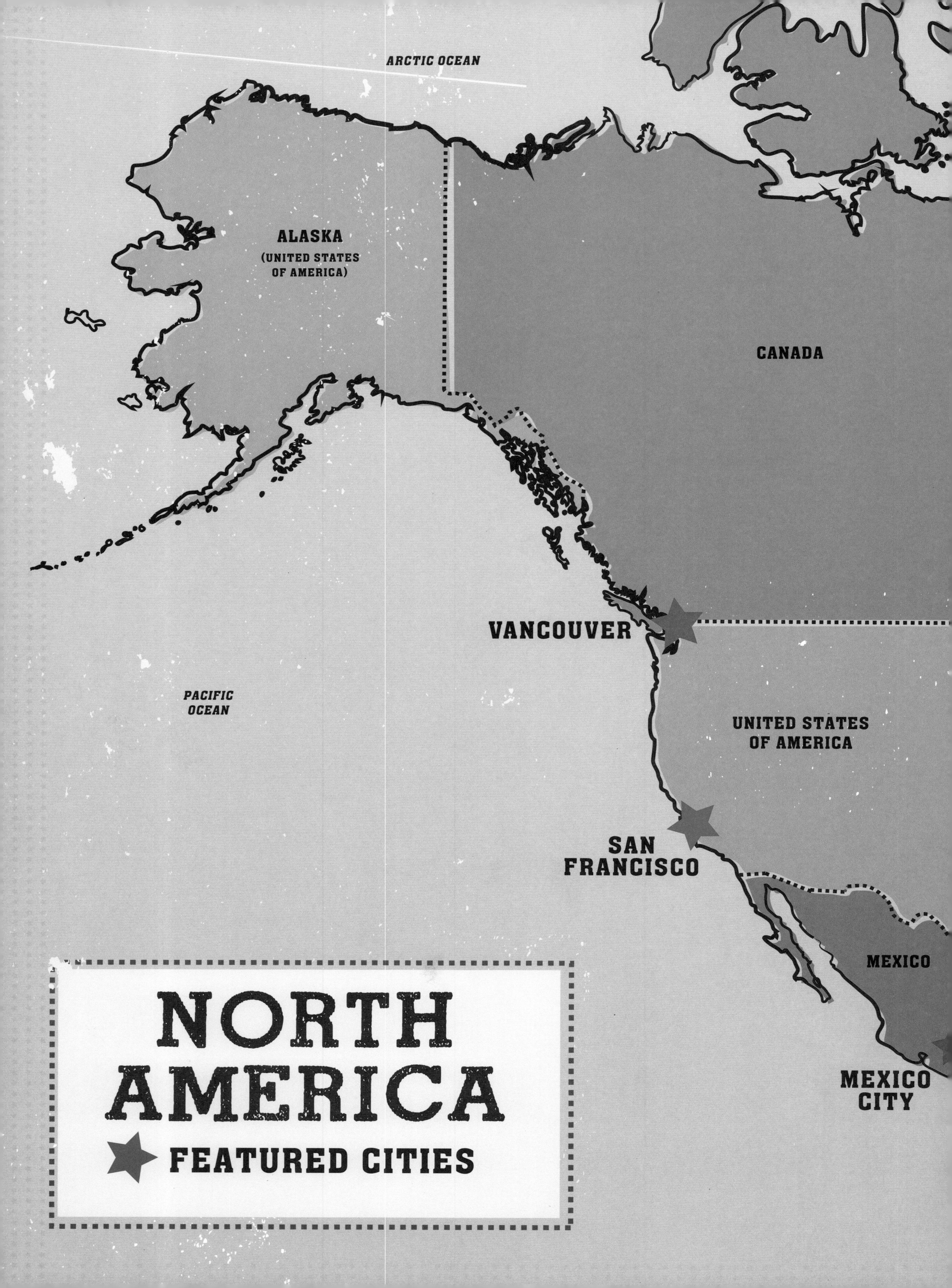

ARCTIC OCEAN
ALASKA
(UNITED STATES
OF AMERICA)
CANADA
VANCOUVER
PACIFIC
OCEAN
UNITED STATES
OF AMERICA
SAN
FRANCISCO
MEXICO
MEXICO
CITY
NORTH
AMERICA
FEATURED CITIES

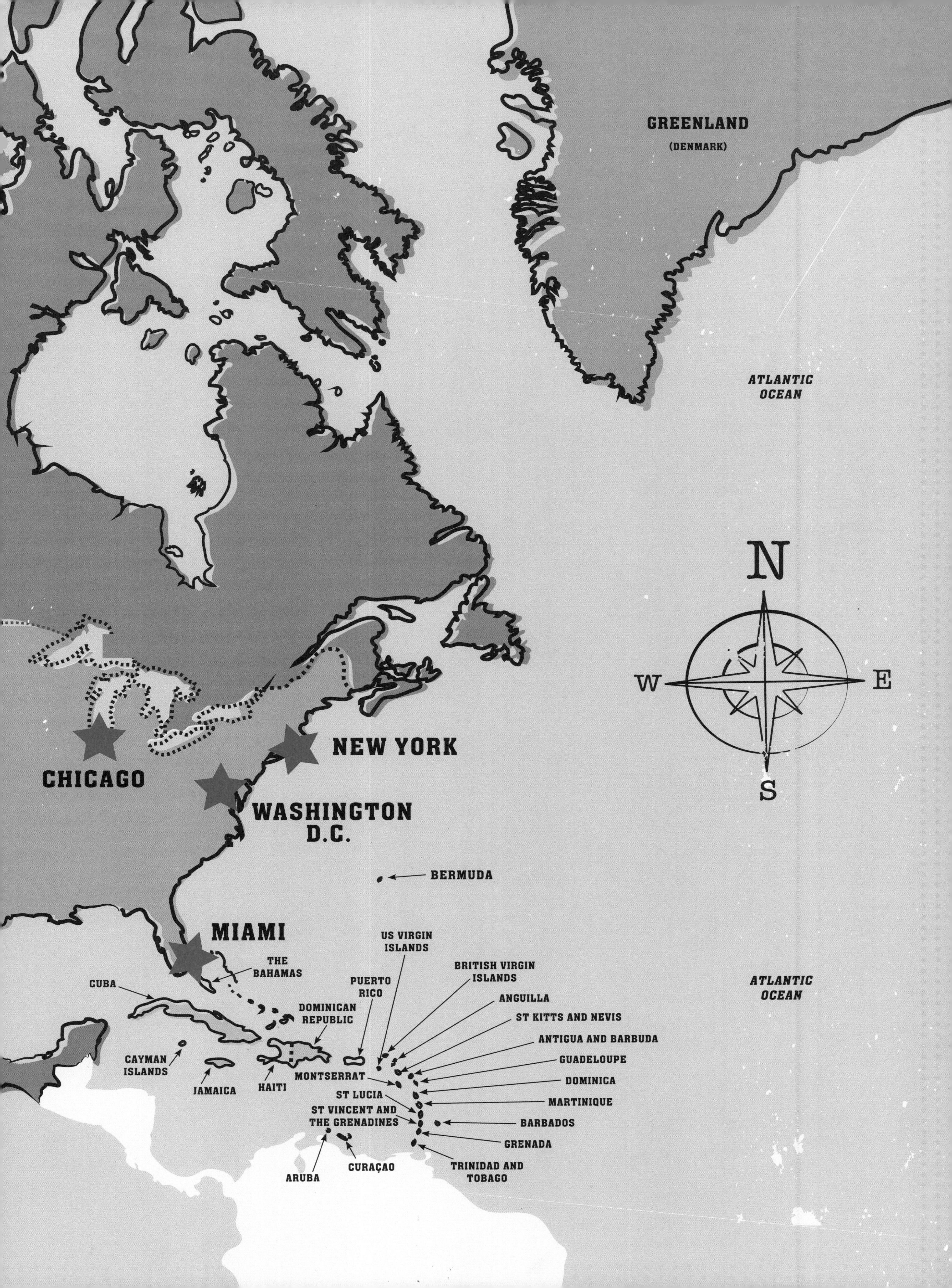
GREENLAND
(DENMARK)
ATLANTIC
OCEAN
N
W
E
S
NEW YORK
CHICAGO
WASHINGTON
D.C.
BERMUDA
MIAMI
US VIRGIN
ISLANDS
BRITISH VIRGIN
ISLANDS
THE
BAHAMAS
PUERTO
RICO
CUBA
ANGUILLA
ATLANTIC
OCEAN
DOMINICAN
REPUBLIC
ST KITTS AND NEVIS
ANTIGUA AND BARBUDA
CAYMAN
ISLANDS
GUADELOUPE
MONTSERRAT
DOMINICA
JAMAICA
HAITI
ST LUCIA
MARTINIQUE
ST VINCENT AND
THE GRENADINES
BARBADOS
GRENADA
ARUBA
CURAÇAO
TRINIDAD AND
TOBAGO

VANCOUVER

Surrounded by ocean, mountains and sweeping forests, this Canadian city boasts amazing views and some incredible animal sightings. It is one of the cleanest cities in the world, and the birthplace of the Greenpeace movement, which aims to protect the environment around the globe. Bears, bald eagles and beavers can be seen around the city, while the coastline is a hotspot for orcas, seals and even grey whales.

The nesting colony of **great blue herons** in Stanley Park is one of the biggest in North America.

Great blue heron

STANLEY PARK

Grey whale

Orca

Surf scoter

Bushtit

ENGLISH BAY

HARBOUR CENTRE

DOWNTOWN

BC PLACE

JERICHO BEACH PARK

North American beaver

WRECK BEACH

River otter

OLYMPIC VILLAGE

Tree frog

Vancouver's Olympic Village and the wetlands around it have recently become home to a family of **beavers**.

Steller sea lion

PACIFIC SPIRIT PARK

River otters frolic in the city's rivers while sea otters – nearly hunted to extinction – are making a comeback off the coast. They can also be seen at the aquarium.

Black bear

QUEEN ELIZABETH PARK

VANDUSEN BOTANICAL GARDEN

See exotic birds at the Bloedel Conservatory in Queen Elizabeth Park.

Black-capped chickadee

Striped skunk

THE BLACK BEAR BIN-MAN

ANIMAL STORIES

Medium-sized black bears roam the woods outside Vancouver – and very rarely they are spotted entering the city, probably to look for food. But in 2011 one bear's quest for a snack took him on an adventure nobody could have imagined . . .

While the bear was raiding a skip for food, the whole skip – with the bear still inside it – was picked up by a rubbish truck and driven away. The bear managed to climb onto the roof of the vehicle, where it was photographed 'surfing' down the street!

Luckily the bear was soon rescued and released back into the wild.

Harbour seals swim up to 500km up the Fraser River. Some fishermen blame them for reduced salmon numbers.

American crow

Harbour seal

FRASER RIVER

RICHMOND

Little brown bat
Northern flying squirrel
Oystercatcher
Barrow's goldeneye
Western red-backed salamander
AMAZING SPACES
STANLEY PARK
Around 500 species are known to live in Stanley Park, including up to six types of bat. It is an important stopover for migratory birds, with as many as 230 different types sighted here every year.
VANCOUVER HARBOUR
Downy woodpecker
ARCTIC OCEAN
CANADA
ATLANTIC OCEAN
AIRPORT
GREEN SPACES
AQUARIUM
ANIMAL SIGHTINGS
Northern flicker
A bobcat has reportedly been seen roaming the Burnaby suburbs. It is twice the size of a domestic cat.
There are so many Canada geese here that they sometimes pose a risk to passing aeroplanes.
Canada goose
Pacific wren
Bobcat
EAST SIDE
BURNABY
Douglas squirrel
BURNABY LAKE PARK
Rufous hummingbird
DEER LAKE PARK
Western painted turtle
Coyote
Over a dozen bald eagle nests are under observation across Vancouver. In winter, the city dump at the Ladner Landfill, below Richmond, is home to 2,000 bald eagles. They can be spotted perching on tall fence posts or circling the nearby river, looking for prey.
Bald eagle
Over 300 coyotes live in and around Vancouver, but they are rarely seen as they usually come out at night and tend to avoid people.
Can you find the 10 hidden beavers?

SAN FRANCISCO

At the tip of a hilly peninsula on the west coast of the United States, sits the historic city of San Francisco. The city is known for its sea fogs, cable cars and many artists and musicians. Its most famous landmarks are the Golden Gate Bridge and Alcatraz Island, which was once home to a notorious prison. The waters around San Francisco are fantastic for spotting marine life such as porpoises, dolphins and migrating whales.

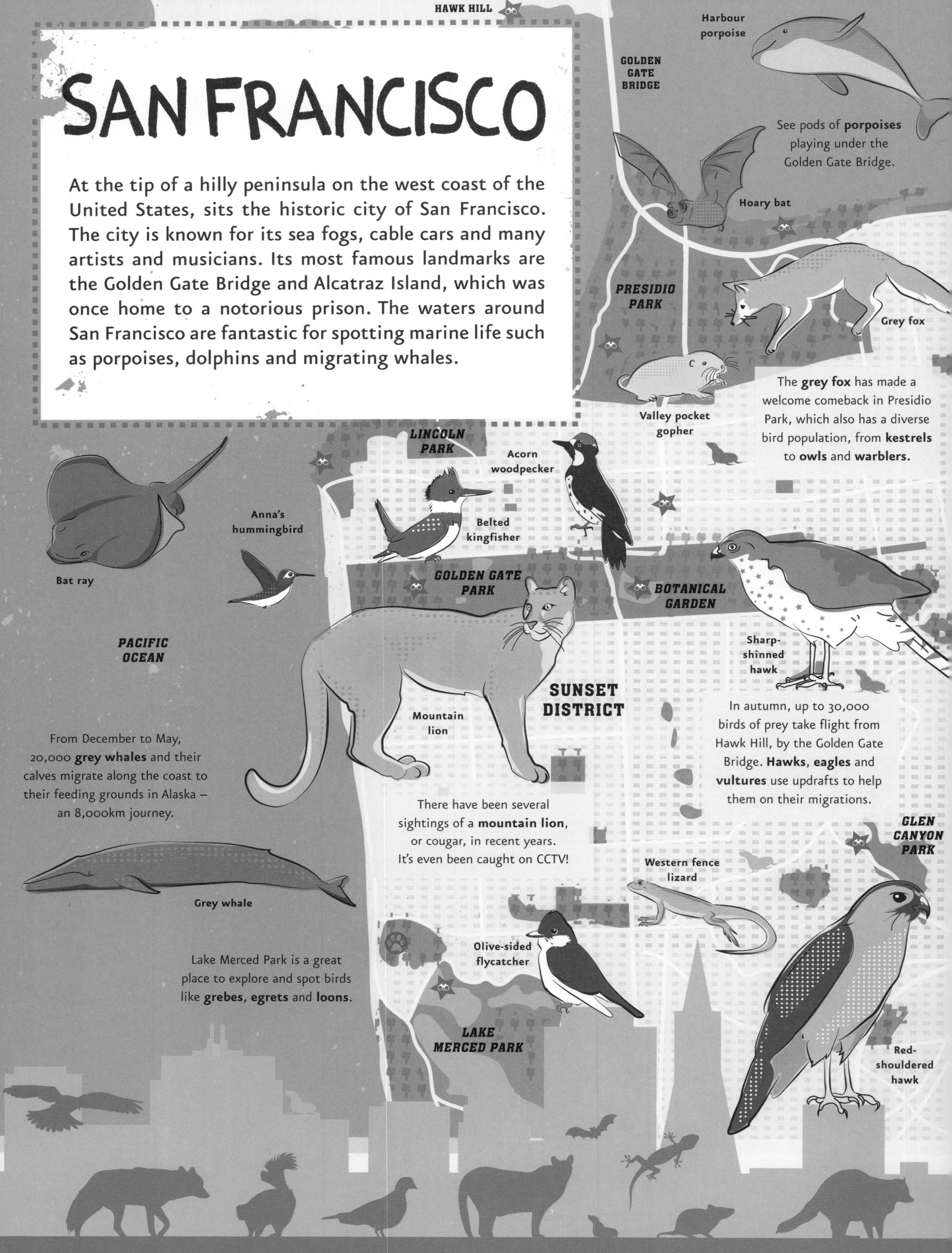

See pods of **porpoises** playing under the Golden Gate Bridge.

The **grey fox** has made a welcome comeback in Presidio Park, which also has a diverse bird population, from **kestrels** to **owls** and **warblers.**

In autumn, up to 30,000 birds of prey take flight from Hawk Hill, by the Golden Gate Bridge. **Hawks**, **eagles** and **vultures** use updrafts to help them on their migrations.

From December to May, 20,000 **grey whales** and their calves migrate along the coast to their feeding grounds in Alaska – an 8,000km journey.

There have been several sightings of a **mountain lion**, or cougar, in recent years. It's even been caught on CCTV!

Lake Merced Park is a great place to explore and spot birds like **grebes**, **egrets** and **loons**.

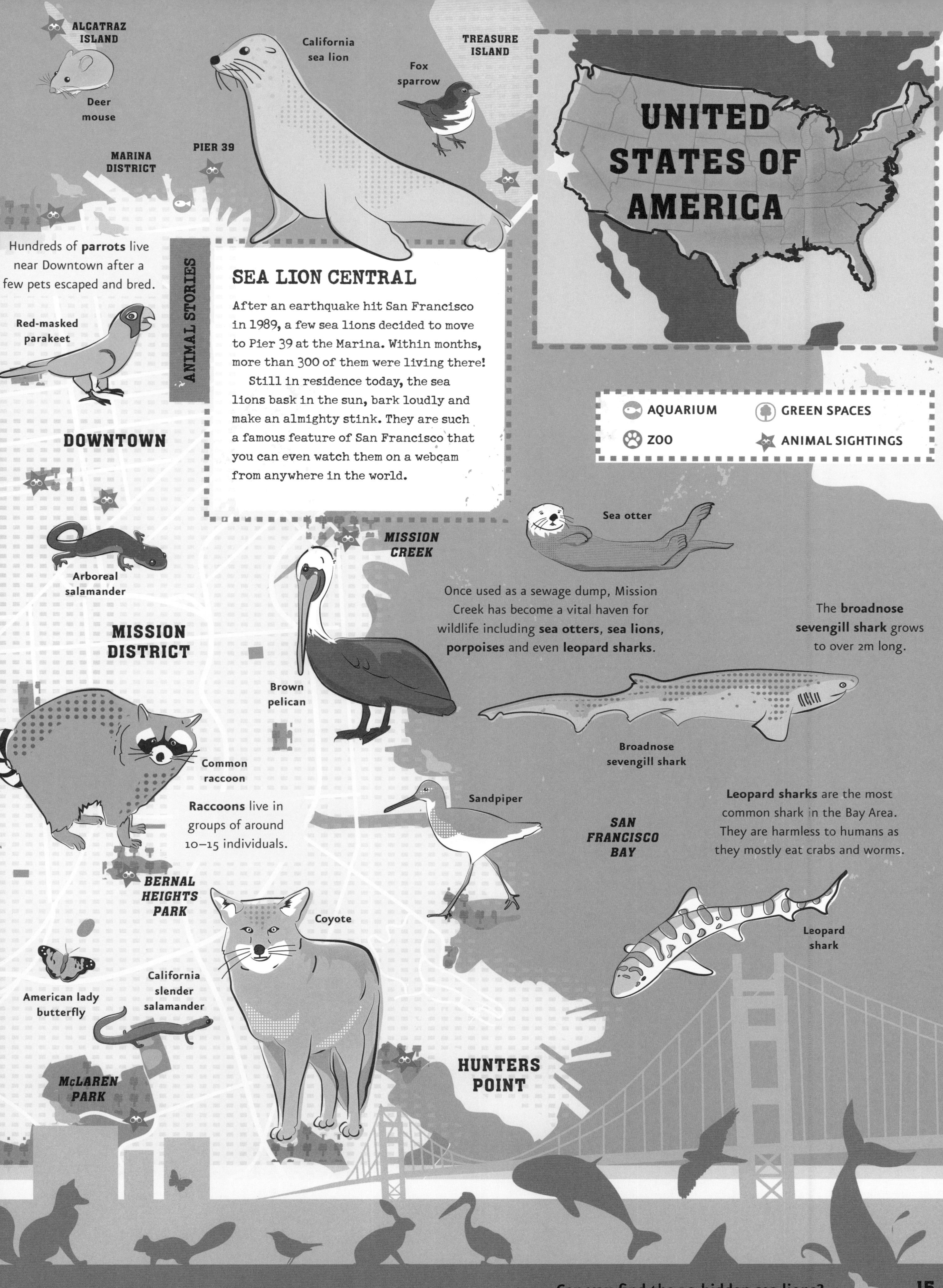

SEA LION CENTRAL

After an earthquake hit San Francisco in 1989, a few sea lions decided to move to Pier 39 at the Marina. Within months, more than 300 of them were living there!

Still in residence today, the sea lions bask in the sun, bark loudly and make an almighty stink. They are such a famous feature of San Francisco that you can even watch them on a webcam from anywhere in the world.

Can you find the 10 hidden sea lions?

CHICAGO

The city of Chicago is the largest city in the Midwestern United States and the third biggest in the country. Perched on the southwest shore of Lake Michigan, it is famed for its skyscrapers – though their lights can disrupt the flight paths of migrating birds. However, Chicago's 'Lights Out' programme, encouraging building owners to turn off lights during migration season, is thought to save 10,000 birds a year!

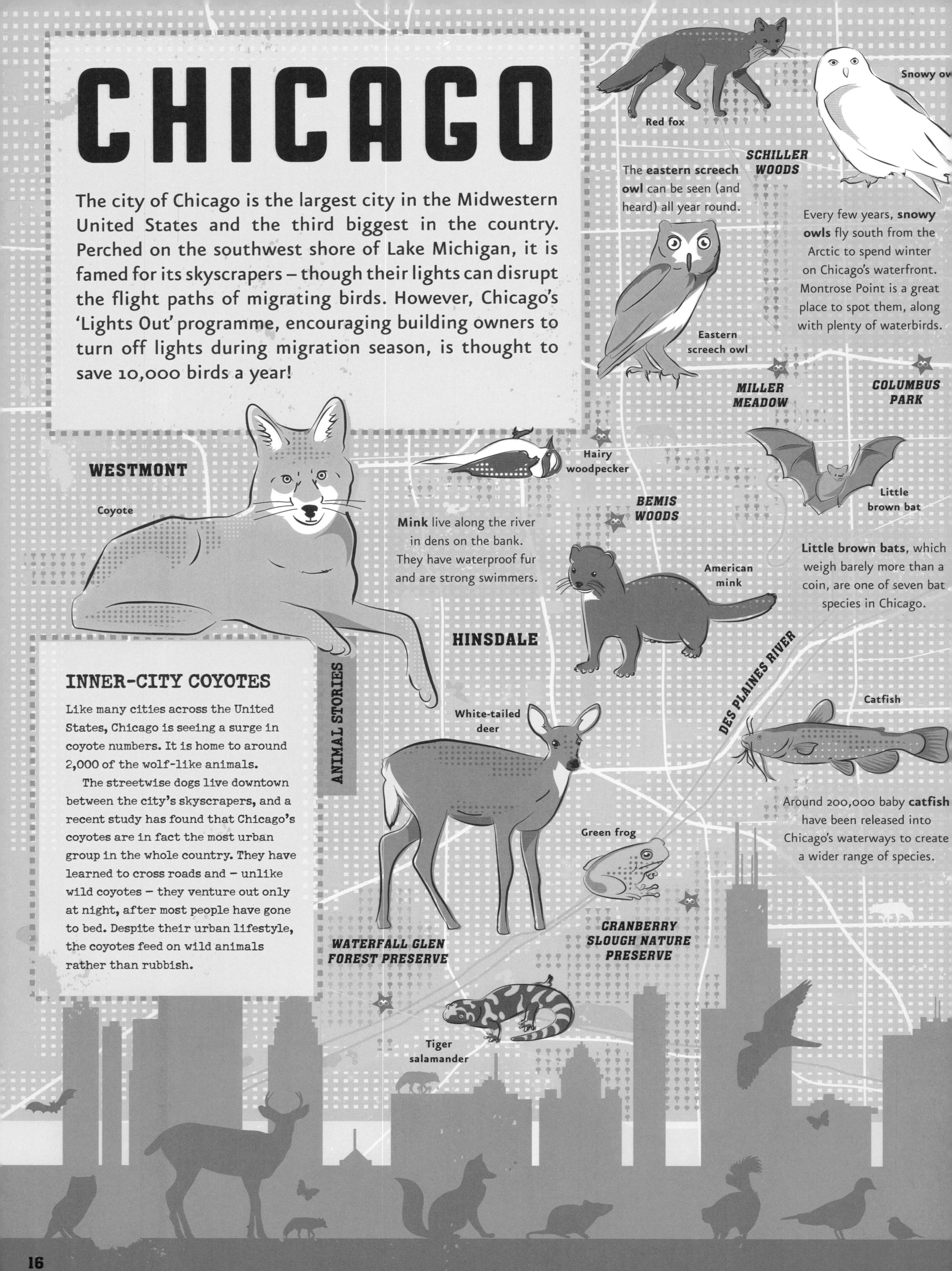

Red fox

Snowy owl

SCHILLER WOODS

The **eastern screech owl** can be seen (and heard) all year round.

Every few years, **snowy owls** fly south from the Arctic to spend winter on Chicago's waterfront. Montrose Point is a great place to spot them, along with plenty of waterbirds.

Eastern screech owl

MILLER MEADOW

COLUMBUS PARK

WESTMONT

Coyote

Hairy woodpecker

Little brown bat

BEMIS WOODS

Mink live along the river in dens on the bank. They have waterproof fur and are strong swimmers.

American mink

Little brown bats, which weigh barely more than a coin, are one of seven bat species in Chicago.

HINSDALE

DES PLAINES RIVER

INNER-CITY COYOTES

Like many cities across the United States, Chicago is seeing a surge in coyote numbers. It is home to around 2,000 of the wolf-like animals.

The streetwise dogs live downtown between the city's skyscrapers, and a recent study has found that Chicago's coyotes are in fact the most urban group in the whole country. They have learned to cross roads and – unlike wild coyotes – they venture out only at night, after most people have gone to bed. Despite their urban lifestyle, the coyotes feed on wild animals rather than rubbish.

ANIMAL STORIES

White-tailed deer

Catfish

Around 200,000 baby **catfish** have been released into Chicago's waterways to create a wider range of species.

Green frog

CRANBERRY SLOUGH NATURE PRESERVE

WATERFALL GLEN FOREST PRESERVE

Tiger salamander

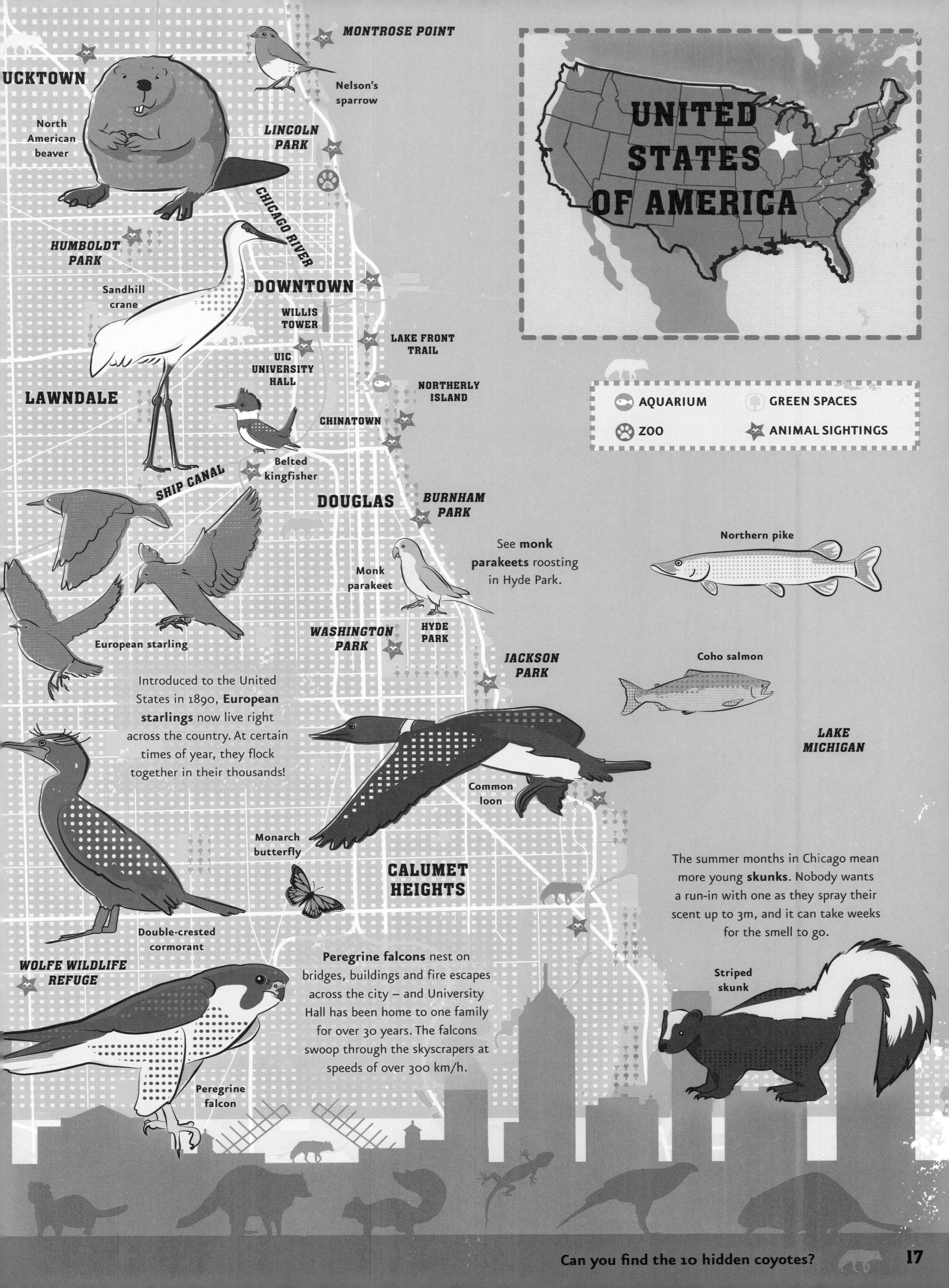
UCKTOWN
MONTROSE POINT
North American beaver
Nelson's sparrow
LINCOLN PARK
CHICAGO RIVER
HUMBOLDT PARK
DOWNTOWN
Sandhill crane
WILLIS TOWER
UIC UNIVERSITY HALL
LAKE FRONT TRAIL
NORTHERLY ISLAND
LAWNDALE
CHINATOWN
Belted kingfisher
SHIP CANAL
DOUGLAS
BURNHAM PARK
UNITED STATES OF AMERICA
AQUARIUM
GREEN SPACES
ZOO
ANIMAL SIGHTINGS
Northern pike
See **monk parakeets** roosting in Hyde Park.
Monk parakeet
HYDE PARK
WASHINGTON PARK
European starling
JACKSON PARK
Coho salmon
Introduced to the United States in 1890, **European starlings** now live right across the country. At certain times of year, they flock together in their thousands!
LAKE MICHIGAN
Common loon
Monarch butterfly
CALUMET HEIGHTS
The summer months in Chicago mean more young **skunks**. Nobody wants a run-in with one as they spray their scent up to 3m, and it can take weeks for the smell to go.
Double-crested cormorant
WOLFE WILDLIFE REFUGE
Peregrine falcons nest on bridges, buildings and fire escapes across the city – and University Hall has been home to one family for over 30 years. The falcons swoop through the skyscrapers at speeds of over 300 km/h.
Striped skunk
Peregrine falcon
Can you find the 10 hidden coyotes?

NEW YORK

Home to more than 8 million people, New York City is the biggest city in the United States – and one of the greenest in the country, too. In the heart of Manhattan Island, surrounded by skyscrapers, Central Park boasts over 270 species of wildlife! Elsewhere you can see skunks in Harlem, find wild turkeys on the streets of Staten Island and, if you're really lucky, you might just spot a humpback whale coming up for air in the Upper Bay.

A pair of baby **skunks** was once rescued from a station in the Bronx.

Striped skunk

Coyotes have been spotted in the heart of Manhattan – even on a rooftop bar!

Coyote

HUDSON HEIGHTS

HARLEM

Great horned owl

CENTRAL PARK

Yellow-bellied sapsucker

EMPIRE STATE BUILDING

CHRYSLER BUILDING

MANHATTAN

BROOKLYN BRIDGE

ONE WORLD TRADE CENTER

Grey squirrel

STATUE OF LIBERTY

Groundhog

PROSPECT PARK

Common raccoon

GREEN-WOOD CEMETERY

Almost 700 **deer** roam the green spaces of Staten Island. You can also spot **bald eagles** at High Rock Park, and see **feral turkeys** strutting the streets.

White-tailed deer

AMAZING SPACES

Swallowtail butterfly

American goldfinch

Cooter turtle

Catfish

CENTRAL PARK

Central Park is a huge green space in the heart of the city, with several ponds, a zoo, a wildlife sanctuary and even woodland. Look out for great horned owls and scampering chipmunks.

Freshkills Park used to be the biggest landfill in the world. It is now being turned into a wildlife park.

UPPER BAY

Green-Wood Cemetery is the largest in the city and is home to at least 216 bird species.

Bald eagle

Wild turkey

SILVER LAKE PARK

BROOKLYN

Fisher

Monk parakeet

STATEN ISLAND

FRESHKILLS PARK

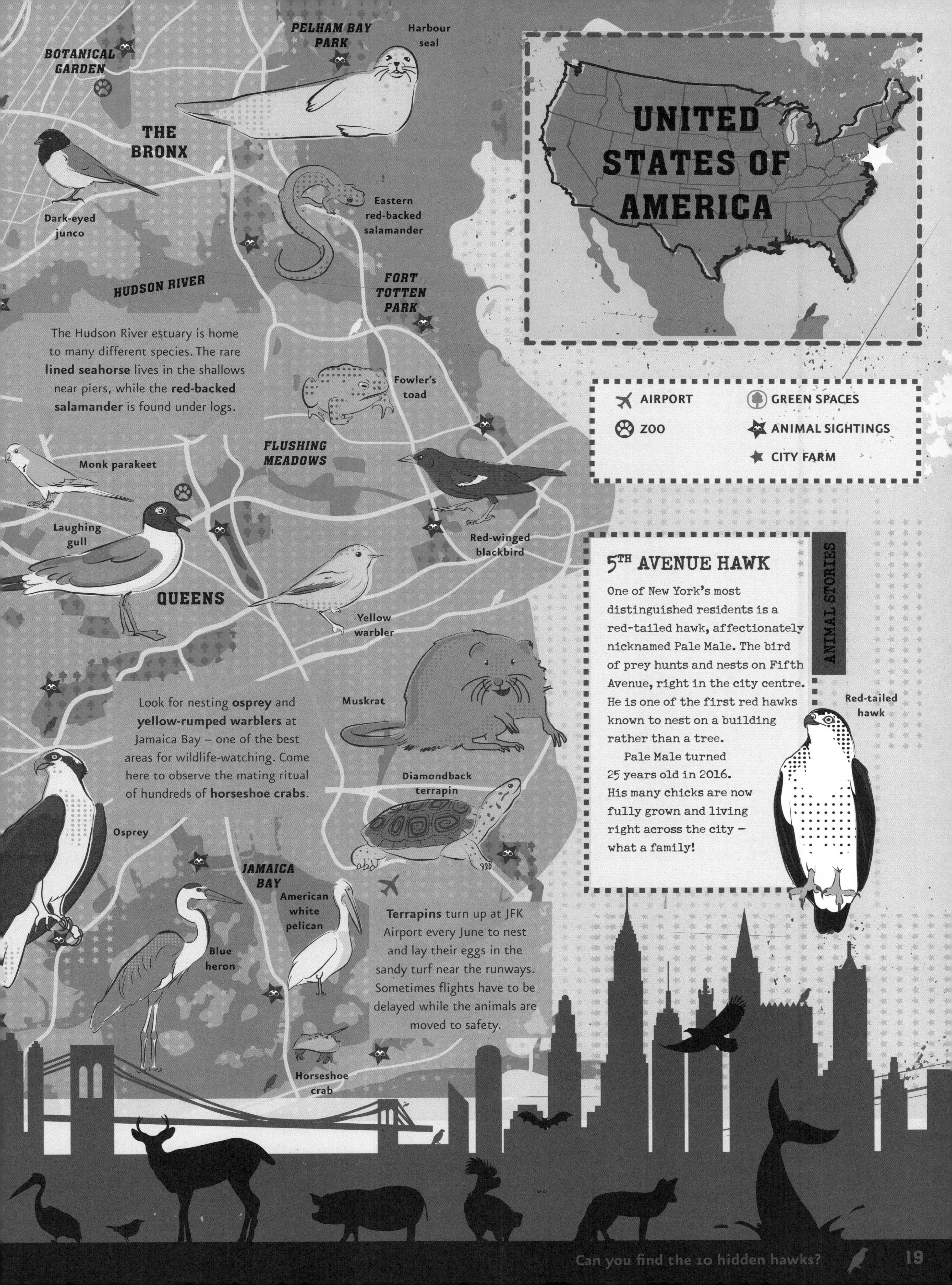

The Hudson River estuary is home to many different species. The rare **lined seahorse** lives in the shallows near piers, while the **red-backed salamander** is found under logs.

Look for nesting **osprey** and **yellow-rumped warblers** at Jamaica Bay – one of the best areas for wildlife-watching. Come here to observe the mating ritual of hundreds of **horseshoe crabs**.

Terrapins turn up at JFK Airport every June to nest and lay their eggs in the sandy turf near the runways. Sometimes flights have to be delayed while the animals are moved to safety.

ANIMAL STORIES

5TH AVENUE HAWK

One of New York's most distinguished residents is a red-tailed hawk, affectionately nicknamed Pale Male. The bird of prey hunts and nests on Fifth Avenue, right in the city centre. He is one of the first red hawks known to nest on a building rather than a tree.

Pale Male turned 25 years old in 2016. His many chicks are now fully grown and living right across the city – what a family!

Can you find the 10 hidden hawks?

WASHINGTON D.C.

Washington D.C. is the home of the President of the United States and is the nation's capital city. Its elegant classical buildings, including the famous White House, Capitol and Supreme Court, are the centres of the US government. Sited on the junction of the scenic Potomac and Anacostia Rivers, this political powerhouse still boasts plenty of thriving wildlife from migrating birds to a friendly local fox.

Thousands of birds migrate through Rock Creek National Park every spring and autumn.

NATIONAL ZOOLOGICAL PARK

Black-crowned night heron

McMILLAN RESERVOIR

Black-crowned night herons gather every summer at the city zoo, where they breed and steal a few free fish!

Ruby-crowned kinglet

GLEBE ROAD PARK

Wood thrush

WHITEHAVEN PARKWAY

POTOMAC OVERLOOK REGIONAL PARK

GEORGETOWN

DOWNTOWN

The **catbird** makes a sound like a 'miaow'!

Grey catbird

THE WHITE HOUSE

Baltimore oriole

ROSSLYN

Virginia opossum

LINCOLN MEMORIAL

WASHINGTON MONUMENT

Virginia opossums come out at night looking for food, and they'll eat anything from poisonous snakes to cockroaches! When threatened, they are known to play dead or 'play possum' to put off an attacker.

Eastern grey squirrel

ARLINGTON NATIONAL CEMETERY

ARLINGTON

Killdeer

Southern flying squirrel

THE PENTAGON

POTOMAC RIVER

EAST POTOMAC PARK

Long Branch Park is one of the best places in the world to see **flying squirrels**, which can glide over 40m.

HAINS POINT

LONG BRANCH NATURE CENTER AND PARK

Cooper's hawk

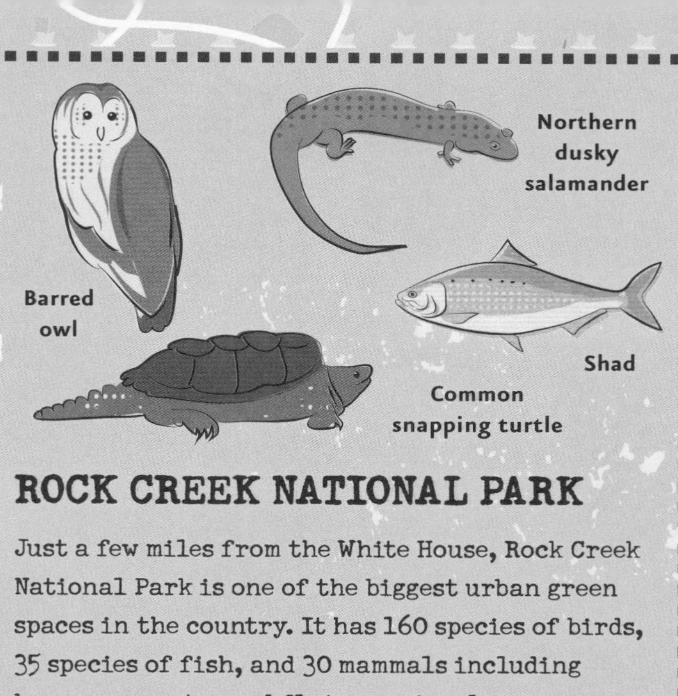

ROCK CREEK NATIONAL PARK

Just a few miles from the White House, Rock Creek National Park is one of the biggest urban green spaces in the country. It has 160 species of birds, 35 species of fish, and 30 mammals including beavers, coyotes and flying squirrels.

Ruby-throated hummingbird

The **ruby-throated hummingbird** – often spotted in gardens – beats its wings 53 times a second.

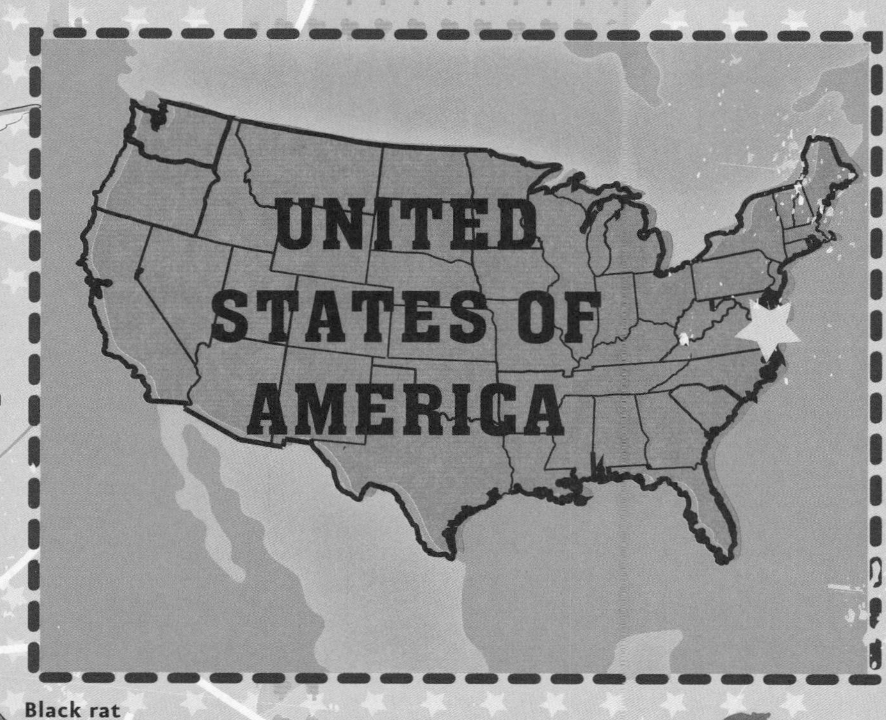

Black rat snake

AIRPORT
ZOO
GREEN SPACES
ANIMAL SIGHTINGS
CITY FARM

WOODRIDGE

White-tailed deer

COLMAR MANOR COMMUNITY PARK

KENILWORTH PARK AND AQUATIC GARDENS

Eastern cottontail rabbit

UNITED STATES NATIONAL ARBORETUM

CHEVERLY

Chimney swift

Wood duck

NORTHEAST WASHINGTON

DEANWOOD

American badger

There are plenty of groundhogs in D.C. It is thought that if you can see one's shadow on 2 February, or Groundhog Day, there will be six more weeks of winter.

FORT CHAPLIN PARK

CAPITOL HILL

Groundhog

FORT CIRCLE PARK

Northern cardinal

A **red fox** became famous in 2014, when frequent sightings led to him being nicknamed the 'Capitol Hill fox'.

Red fox

JOSIAH THE BADGER

The White House is the official home of the President, but did you know it has also been home to many animals over the years? Presidential pets have included cats and dogs, but also lions, bears and even a badger!

Theodore Roosevelt (1901–09) owned a grumpy badger called Josiah, who would try to bite unsuspecting staff. And during World War I, Woodrow Wilson (1913–21) brought a flock of sheep in to trim the White House lawns – this saved manpower and raised $52,823 for charity when their wool was auctioned.

MIAMI

Situated near the southern tip of Florida, Miami is a major tourist destination, known for its Art Deco buildings, white sandy beaches and glamorous inhabitants. Since the city borders two national parks and the Atlantic Ocean, it is a hotspot for resident and migrating wildlife. Its warm climate may also explain the high numbers of invasive species in the area, such as Burmese pythons in the Everglades, and green iguanas in residential areas!

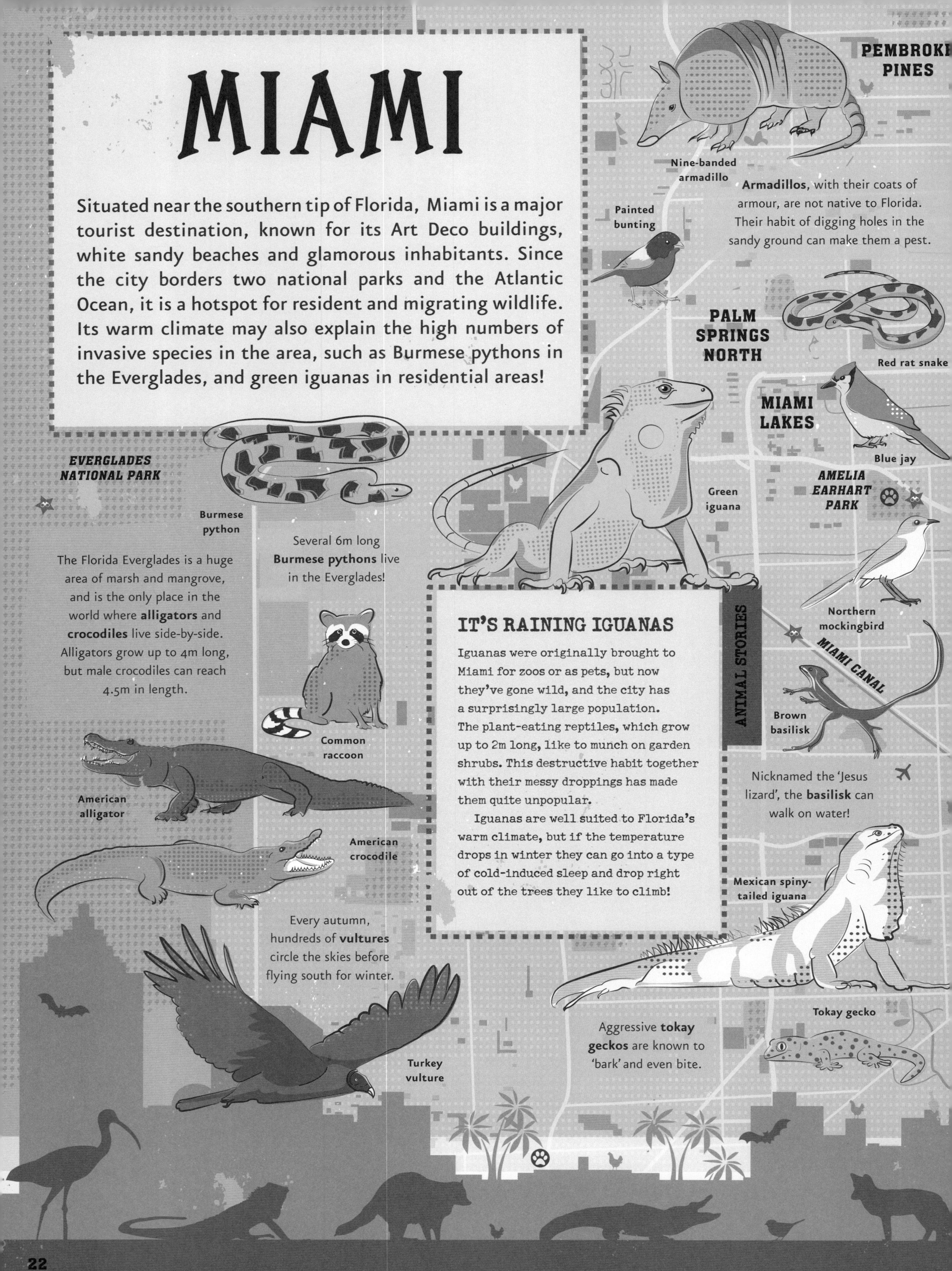

PEMBROKE PINES

Nine-banded armadillo

Armadillos, with their coats of armour, are not native to Florida. Their habit of digging holes in the sandy ground can make them a pest.

Painted bunting

PALM SPRINGS NORTH

Red rat snake

MIAMI LAKES

Blue jay

AMELIA EARHART PARK

Green iguana

EVERGLADES NATIONAL PARK

Burmese python

Several 6m long **Burmese pythons** live in the Everglades!

The Florida Everglades is a huge area of marsh and mangrove, and is the only place in the world where **alligators** and **crocodiles** live side-by-side. Alligators grow up to 4m long, but male crocodiles can reach 4.5m in length.

Northern mockingbird

MIAMI CANAL

Common raccoon

American alligator

American crocodile

IT'S RAINING IGUANAS

ANIMAL STORIES

Iguanas were originally brought to Miami for zoos or as pets, but now they've gone wild, and the city has a surprisingly large population. The plant-eating reptiles, which grow up to 2m long, like to munch on garden shrubs. This destructive habit together with their messy droppings has made them quite unpopular.

Iguanas are well suited to Florida's warm climate, but if the temperature drops in winter they can go into a type of cold-induced sleep and drop right out of the trees they like to climb!

Brown basilisk

Nicknamed the 'Jesus lizard', the **basilisk** can walk on water!

Mexican spiny-tailed iguana

Every autumn, hundreds of **vultures** circle the skies before flying south for winter.

Tokay gecko

Aggressive **tokay geckos** are known to 'bark' and even bite.

Turkey vulture

The ibis is the mascot of the University of Miami. It is famed for its bravery because it is the last bird to seek shelter before a hurricane hits, and the first to come out again afterwards.
American white ibis
UNITED STATES OF AMERICA
Giant African land snail
The invasive giant African land snail is the size of a human hand. It can eat almost everything, even the walls of houses!
NORTH MIAMI BEACH
OLETA RIVER STATE PARK
Grey fox
Grey foxes, raccoons, opossums, dolphins and waterbirds can all be seen at Oleta River State Park.
AIRPORT
GREEN SPACES
ZOO
ANIMAL SIGHTINGS
AQUARIUM
One parrotfish can poo 360kg of sand every year!
Parrotfish
MIAMI SHORES
Royal tern
Feral chickens
LITTLE HAITI
Crowds of feral chickens roam Miami's streets!
Sunbathe with flocks of terns along Miami Beach.
West Indian manatee
West Indian manatees find refuge in the Oleta River State Park. They head south every winter in search of warmer waters.
ATLANTIC OCEAN
American flamingo
MIAMI BEACH
VENETIAN ISLANDS
DODGE ISLAND
MIAMI TOWER
LITTLE HAVANA
FISHER ISLAND
Blacktip shark
Blacktip sharks visit Florida waters in their thousands every January.
VIRGINIA KEY
Sea turtles lay their eggs on beaches around Crandon Park.
CRANDON PARK
Loggerhead sea turtle
Bottlenose dolphin
Can you find the 10 hidden chickens?

MEXICO CITY

The capital city of Mexico sits at a high altitude, up to 2,450m above sea level. Famous for its historic buildings, spicy food, dramatic festivals and folk music, it is one of the largest urban areas in the world, with one of the world's biggest urban parks. The city's wetlands are home to unique and fascinating species, while the volcanoes south of the city are inhabited by the smallest rabbit in the world – the endangered volcano rabbit.

Ring-tailed cats can climb head-first down trees and rocks.

Harris's hawks have lived here for three decades after escaping from captivity. They can be seen hunting in groups called 'kettles'.

El Pedregal de San Ángel is bursting with **birds**, **bats** and **rodents**. At the nearby Botanical Gardens you can spot the **cinnamon-bellied flower piercer**, **hummingbirds** and **grosbeaks**.

TARANGO PARK

Volcano rabbits have tiny mouse-like ears, and no tail.

Long-tailed weasel

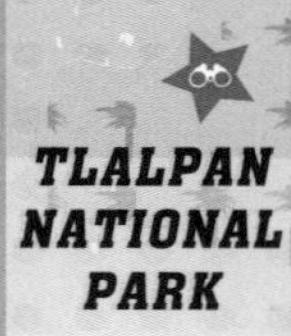

Bronzed cowbird

TLALPAN NATIONAL PARK

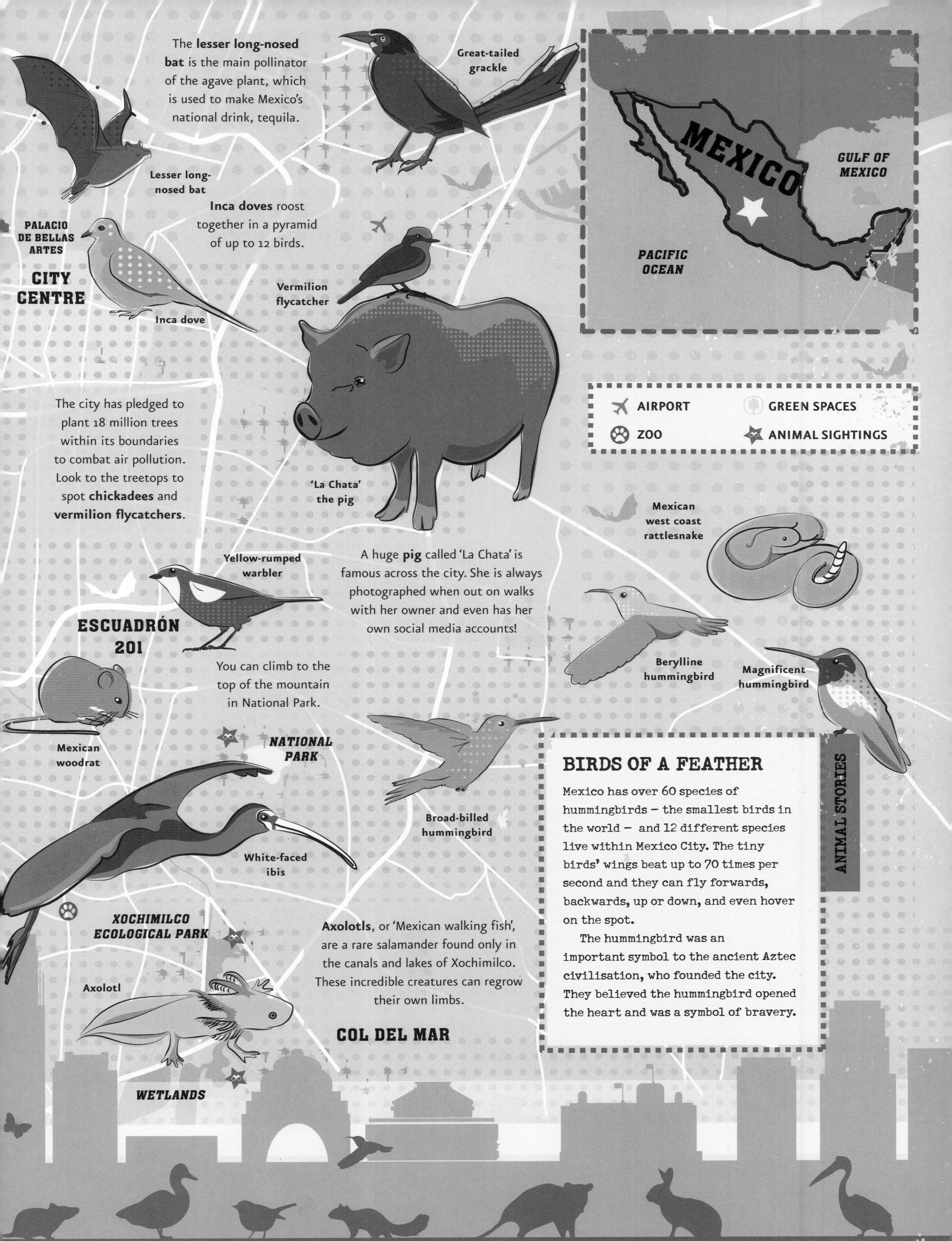

Can you find the 10 hidden bats?

SOUTH AMERICA

The Andes mountains trail down this continent's western shore, while its eastern side boasts one of the longest rivers in the world – the mighty Amazon. Towns and cities here are a haven for exotic species, with sloths in parks, and hummingbirds a common sight in gardens. And with nearly a third of the world's birds found only here, South America is always popular with bird-lovers.

BELIZE
GUATEMALA
HONDURAS
EL SALVADOR
NICARAGUA
PANAMA
COSTA RICA
GUYANA
SURINAME
FRENCH GUIANA
VENEZUELA
COLOMBIA
PANAMA CITY
BOGOTÁ
ECUADOR
PERU
LIMA
BRAZIL
BOLIVIA
CHILE
PARAGUAY
PACIFIC OCEAN
ARGENTINA
URUGUAY
BUENOS AIRES
FALKLAND ISLANDS

ATLANTIC
OCEAN

RIO DE JANEIRO

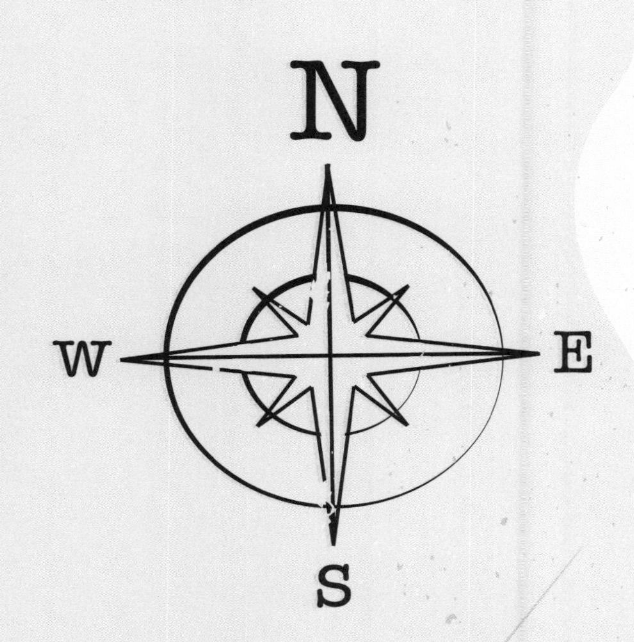

SOUTH AMERICA

★ FEATURED CITIES

SOUTH GEORGIA AND
THE SOUTH SANDWICH
ISLANDS

PANAMA CITY

This bustling city on the Pacific coast is perhaps most famous for the Panama Canal, a 77km-long man-made waterway connecting the Atlantic and Pacific Oceans. Framed by ocean, mangrove forests and tropical rainforest, the city centre is shadowed by towering high-rise buildings. However, despite huge building developments, the city boasts exceptional diversity of plants and animals.

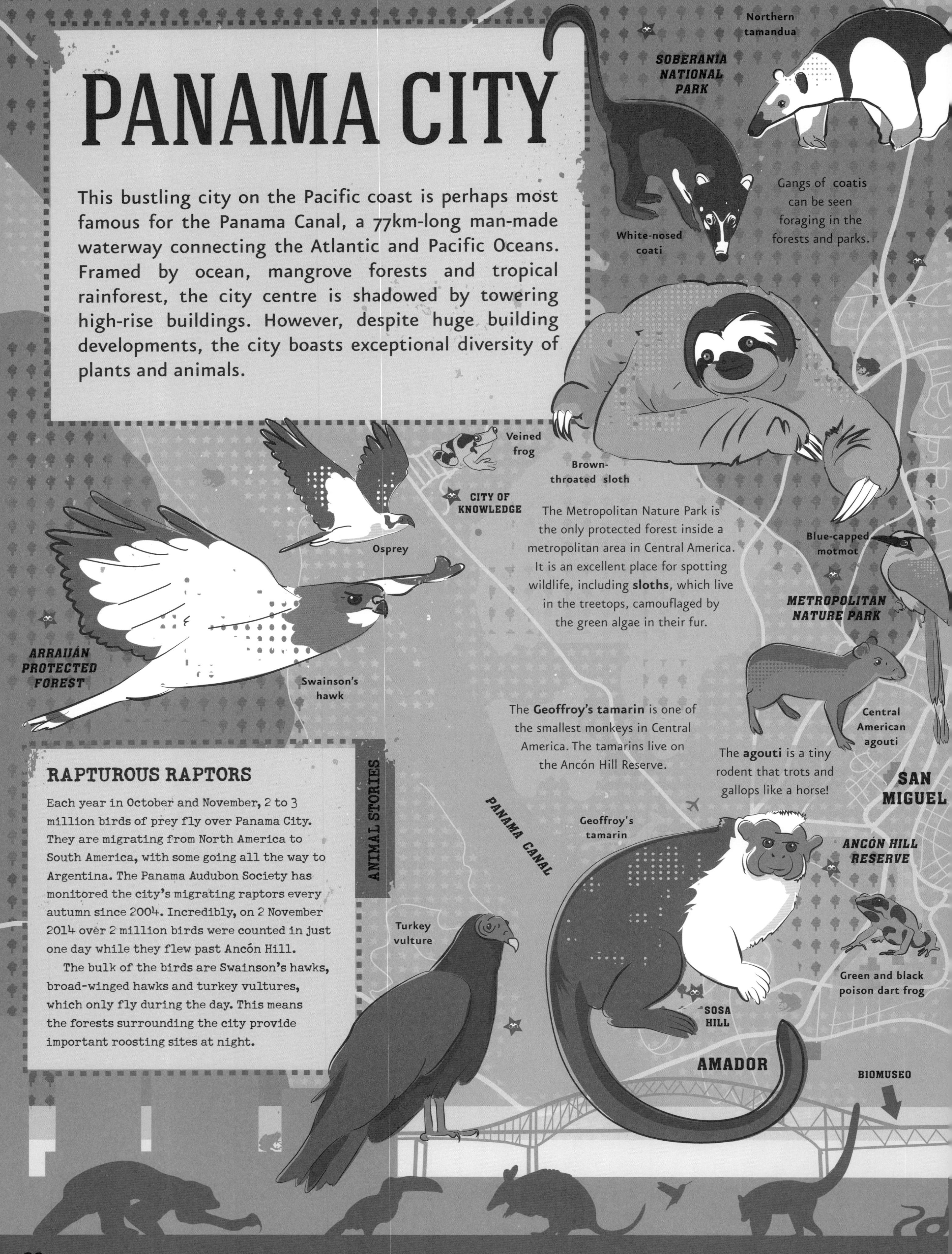

ANIMAL STORIES

RAPTUROUS RAPTORS

Each year in October and November, 2 to 3 million birds of prey fly over Panama City. They are migrating from North America to South America, with some going all the way to Argentina. The Panama Audubon Society has monitored the city's migrating raptors every autumn since 2004. Incredibly, on 2 November 2014 over 2 million birds were counted in just one day while they flew past Ancón Hill.

The bulk of the birds are Swainson's hawks, broad-winged hawks and turkey vultures, which only fly during the day. This means the forests surrounding the city provide important roosting sites at night.

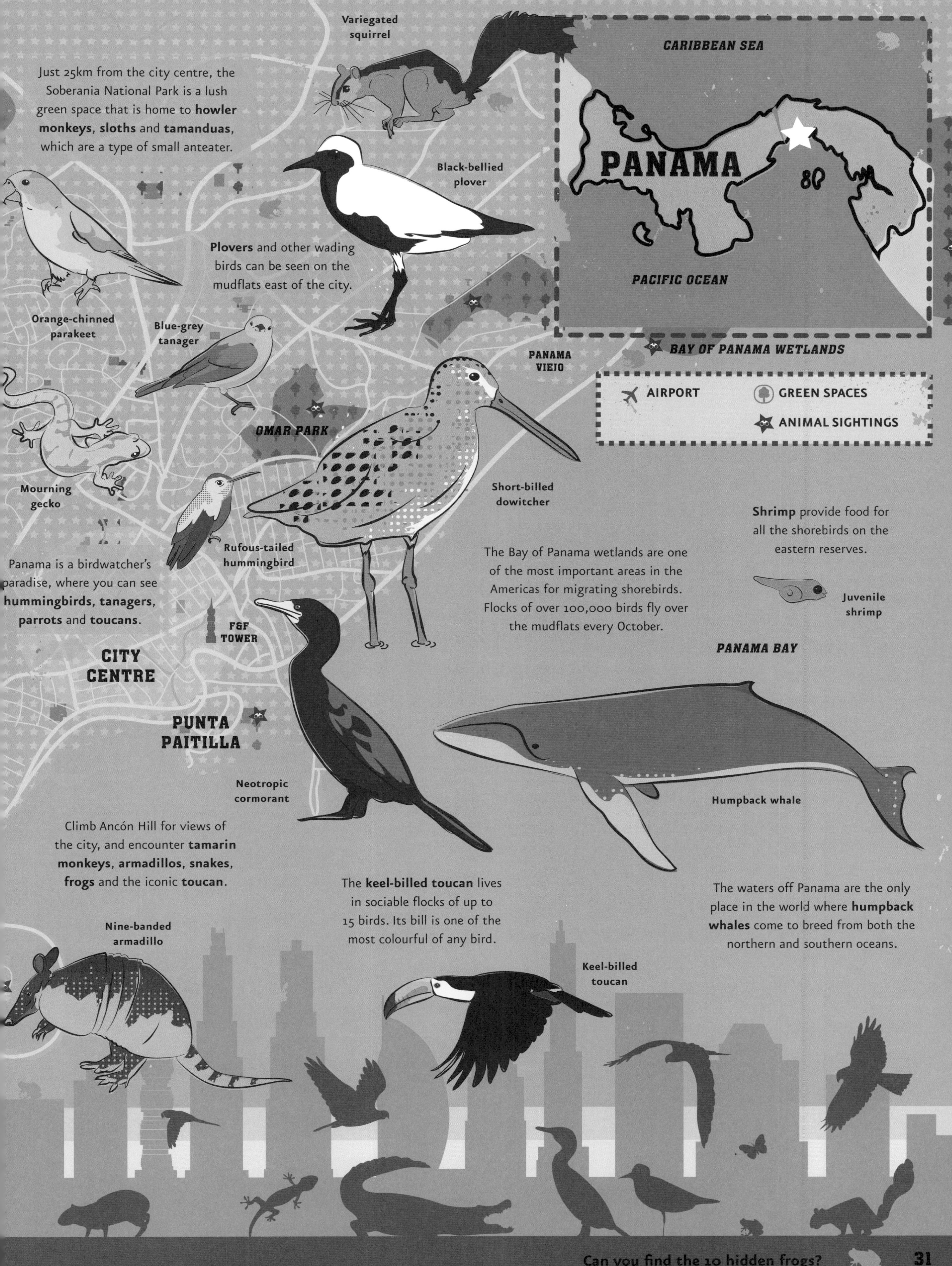
Variegated squirrel
Just 25km from the city centre, the Soberania National Park is a lush green space that is home to **howler monkeys**, **sloths** and **tamanduas**, which are a type of small anteater.
CARIBBEAN SEA
PANAMA
PACIFIC OCEAN
Black-bellied plover
Plovers and other wading birds can be seen on the mudflats east of the city.
Orange-chinned parakeet
Blue-grey tanager
PANAMA VIEJO
BAY OF PANAMA WETLANDS
AIRPORT
GREEN SPACES
ANIMAL SIGHTINGS
OMAR PARK
Mourning gecko
Short-billed dowitcher
Shrimp provide food for all the shorebirds on the eastern reserves.
Rufous-tailed hummingbird
The Bay of Panama wetlands are one of the most important areas in the Americas for migrating shorebirds. Flocks of over 100,000 birds fly over the mudflats every October.
Juvenile shrimp
Panama is a birdwatcher's paradise, where you can see **hummingbirds**, **tanagers**, **parrots** and **toucans**.
F&F TOWER
PANAMA BAY
CITY CENTRE
PUNTA PAITILLA
Neotropic cormorant
Humpback whale
Climb Ancón Hill for views of the city, and encounter **tamarin monkeys**, **armadillos**, **snakes**, **frogs** and the iconic **toucan**.
The **keel-billed toucan** lives in sociable flocks of up to 15 birds. Its bill is one of the most colourful of any bird.
The waters off Panama are the only place in the world where **humpback whales** come to breed from both the northern and southern oceans.
Nine-banded armadillo
Keel-billed toucan
Can you find the 10 hidden frogs?

BOGOTÁ

The capital city of Colombia sits high among the peaks of the Andes Mountains. Its cobblestoned centre is packed with elegant buildings dating back to the days of Spanish rule. In the heart of the city are several wetland areas, preserved to protect their unique wildlife, including species such as the Bogotá rail that are found only in this region. Bogotá is also known for its thriving bat population, and it is home to at least 25 species.

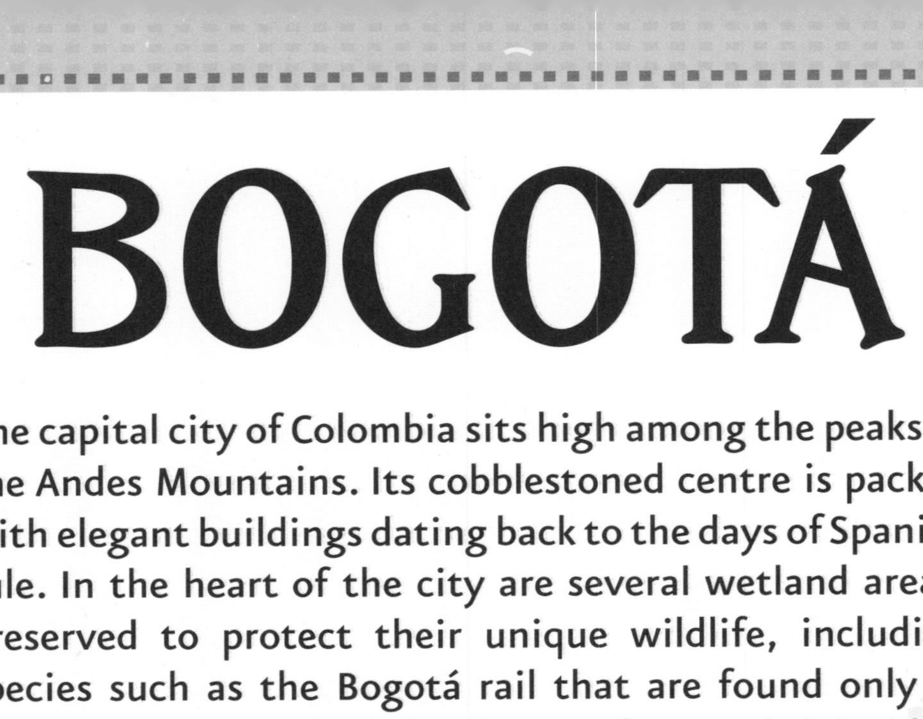

The **red-eared slider turtle** is a widespread invasive species.

The endangered **Apolinar's wren** lives only in Bogotá and the surrounding area.

American coots wade through the shallow waters. They have partially webbed feet that help them to walk on silty land.

The endangered **Bogotá rail** is threatened by the loss of its grassland and wetland habitat. It is easy to identify thanks to its red beak and high-pitched call.

Bogotá is home to around 45,000 **stray dogs** and **cats.** Local police use their time off each week to help the animals by feeding them, worming them and buying them medicine.

There are at least eight species of **hummingbird** across the city, including the **sparkling violetear.**

The **white-tailed kite** can be seen hovering above grassy verges and parks.

SUBA
Wild guinea pigs, known locally as curies, live in the wetlands around Bogotá. They are excellent swimmers.
Guinea pig
Silvery-throated spinetail
Thickhead ground snake
Pied-billed grebe
CÓRDOBA WETLANDS
USAQUÉN
Because of its high altitude and cool temperatures, there are not many reptiles in Bogotá – however, the thickhead ground snake is found around the city's wetlands.
PACIFIC OCEAN
COLOMBIA
AIRPORT
GREEN SPACES
ANIMAL SIGHTINGS
Velvety fruit-eating bat
PARK 93
Rufous-browed conebill
EL VIRREY PARK
BOTANICAL GARDEN
CERROS ORIENTALES
SIMÓN BOLÍVAR METROPOLITAN PARK
Barn owl
Oncilla
Buckley's giant glass frog
Striped owl
Look out for striped and stygian owls in the parks and Botanical Garden, barn owls in the Simón Bolívar Park, and the Andean pygmy owl in the hills.
Threatened with extinction, the giant glass frog can still be found in Bogota's hills.
ANIMAL STORIES
TIGER CAT
The oncilla or 'tiger cat' is a small wild cat from the cloud forests of Central and South America. It is around the same size as a domestic cat, with spots like those of a leopard.
Sadly, years of hunting for its fur, and habitat destruction of the rainforests have left the oncilla in a vulnerable state. The shy cat is rarely seen, but recent reports of one spotted in the Cerros Orientales near Bogotá give some hope for its future.
CITY CENTRE
ENRIQUE OLAYA HERRERA NATIONAL PARK
MONSERRATE
SANTE FE
Western mountain coati
CATHEDRAL OF COLOMBIA
The western mountain coati is found only in Colombia and Ecuador. There have been sightings in the Cerros Orientales.

LIMA

This dry desert city is one of the largest in South America. It has an exciting mix of cultures, with ancient temples, churches built by the Spanish, and modern highrise apartments all set against a backdrop of rugged cliffs and crashing waves. Although Peru is famous for its llamas and alpacas with their soft wool, you won't find many in the city. However, just look up and you'll see hundreds of pelicans and boobies soaring out to sea.

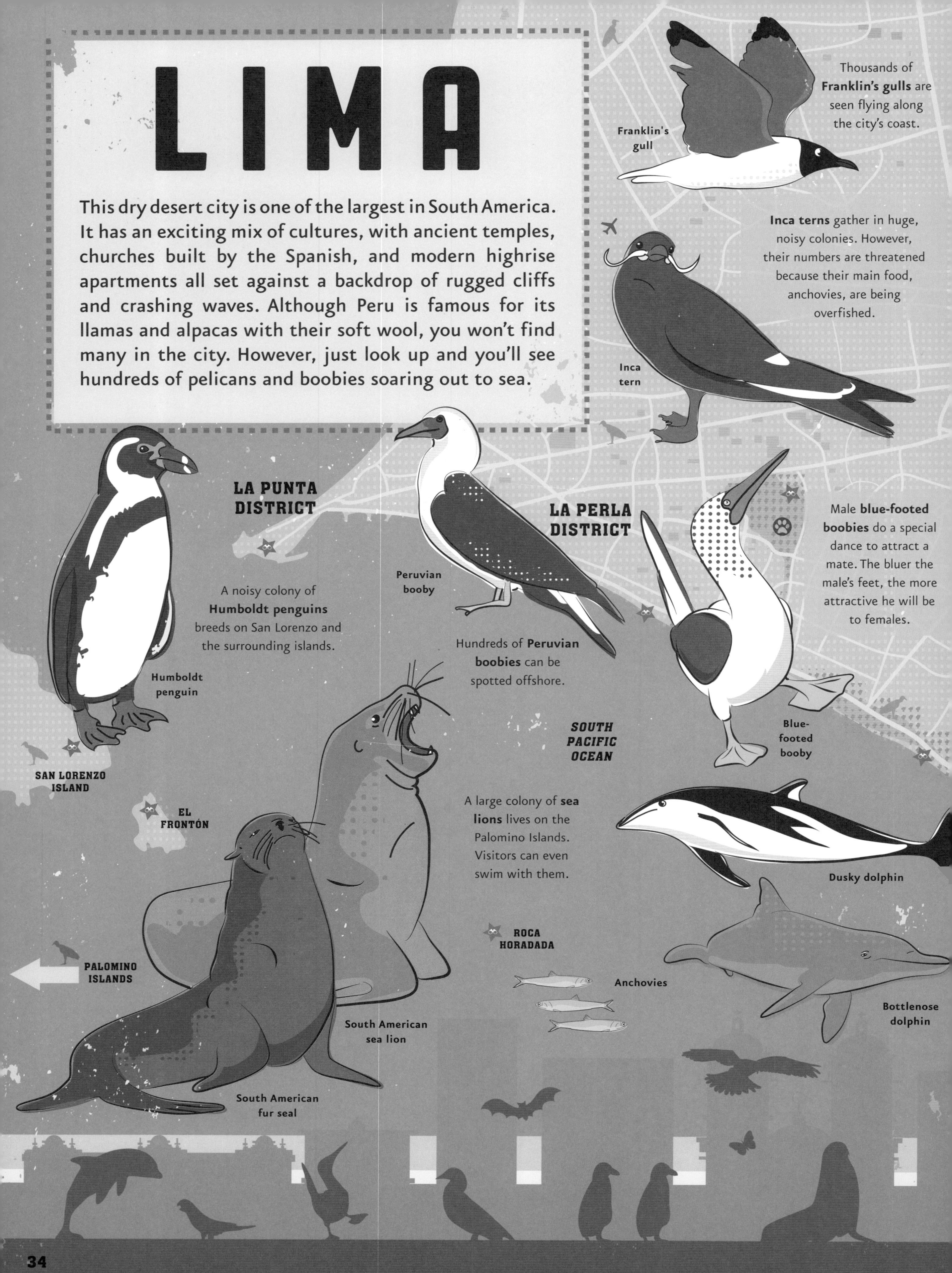

Thousands of **Franklin's gulls** are seen flying along the city's coast.

Franklin's gull

Inca terns gather in huge, noisy colonies. However, their numbers are threatened because their main food, anchovies, are being overfished.

Inca tern

LA PUNTA DISTRICT

LA PERLA DISTRICT

A noisy colony of **Humboldt penguins** breeds on San Lorenzo and the surrounding islands.

Humboldt penguin

Peruvian booby

Hundreds of **Peruvian boobies** can be spotted offshore.

Male **blue-footed boobies** do a special dance to attract a mate. The bluer the male's feet, the more attractive he will be to females.

Blue-footed booby

SOUTH PACIFIC OCEAN

SAN LORENZO ISLAND

EL FRONTÓN

A large colony of **sea lions** lives on the Palomino Islands. Visitors can even swim with them.

Dusky dolphin

ROCA HORADADA

PALOMINO ISLANDS

Anchovies

Bottlenose dolphin

South American sea lion

South American fur seal

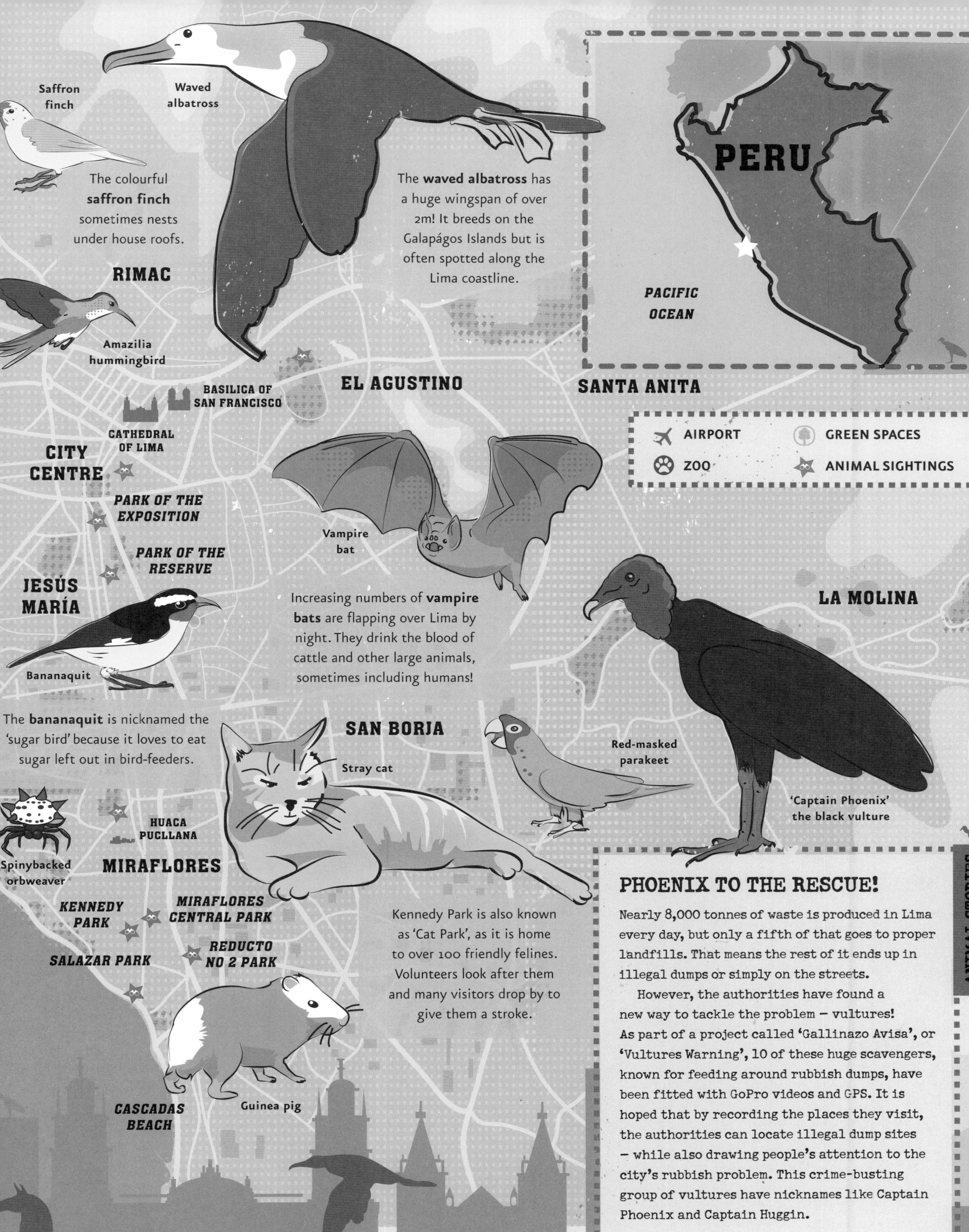

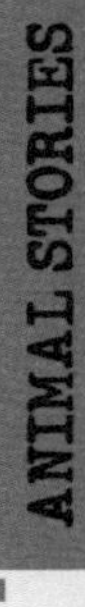

PHOENIX TO THE RESCUE!

Nearly 8,000 tonnes of waste is produced in Lima every day, but only a fifth of that goes to proper landfills. That means the rest of it ends up in illegal dumps or simply on the streets.

However, the authorities have found a new way to tackle the problem – vultures! As part of a project called 'Gallinazo Avisa', or 'Vultures Warning', 10 of these huge scavengers, known for feeding around rubbish dumps, have been fitted with GoPro videos and GPS. It is hoped that by recording the places they visit, the authorities can locate illegal dump sites – while also drawing people's attention to the city's rubbish problem. This crime-busting group of vultures have nicknames like Captain Phoenix and Captain Huggin.

Can you find the 10 hidden vultures?

RIO DE JANEIRO

Rio is a vibrant city with a wild side. Famous for its bright carnivals and samba music, it is fringed by golden beaches and forested mountains. The tallest of these is topped by Christ the Redeemer, a 30m-tall statue and one of the new Seven Wonders of the World. Encasing the city is the partially man-made Tijuca National Park, which is home to thousands of tropical species, from kingsnakes and geckos to coatis, sloths and toucans.

Red-tailed boa constrictor

Red-tailed boa constrictors sometimes enter the favelas (crowded neighbourhoods of shacks) near Tijuca Park.

Rufous-collared sparrow

VILA ISABEL

Common marmoset

Introduced from northern Brazil, **marmosets** are now widespread across the city, living in groups of about 10.

Three-toed sloth

AMAZING SPACES

Green snake

Blue manakin

Crab-eating raccoon

Kingsnake

South American coati

TIJUCA NATIONAL PARK

This urban tropical forest is partly man-made on land once used to grow sugar and coffee. It is home to many rare species, and boasts the famous Christ the Redeemer statue.

PROTECTED AREA

CHRIST THE REDEEMER

Robust woodpecker

LAGE PARK

TIJUCA NATIONAL PARK

ANIMAL STORIES

SLOTH ENCOUNTER

The incredible three-toed sloth spends most its days suspended from the treetops of the Tijuca National Park. Hanging upside down, and sleeping for much of the day, sloths only come down from the treetops once a week in order to go to the toilet. This is when humans are most likely to have a sloth encounter.

Crawling slowly across pathways and roads, the sloths risk traffic accidents, and also make themselves vulnerable to predators. These dangerous trips to the toilet, together with risks to the sloths' forest habitat, means that these animals face an uncertain future.

South American snake-necked turtle

Capybara

BOTANICAL GARDEN

RODRIGO DE FREITAS LAGOON

CIDADE PARK

OLYMPIC GOLF COURSE

At the 2016 Rio Olympics, athletes found the golf course was also home to dozens of **capybaras**, **caimans** and **monkeys**, as well as **burrowing owls**, which make their homes in the sand pits around the course!

MORRO DOIS IRMÃOS

Great white egret

Can you find the 10 hidden marmosets?

BUENOS AIRES

The capital city of Argentina, Buenos Aires sits on the estuary of the Rio de la Plata, where rare dolphins and piranhas swim. It is a city famous for the tango dance, its love of football and its delicious food. Its streets are a mix of tower blocks and European mansions, brightened by vibrant street art. Go downtown and you'll find an incredible reclaimed space called the Costanera Sur Eco Reserve, which is home to some amazing species.

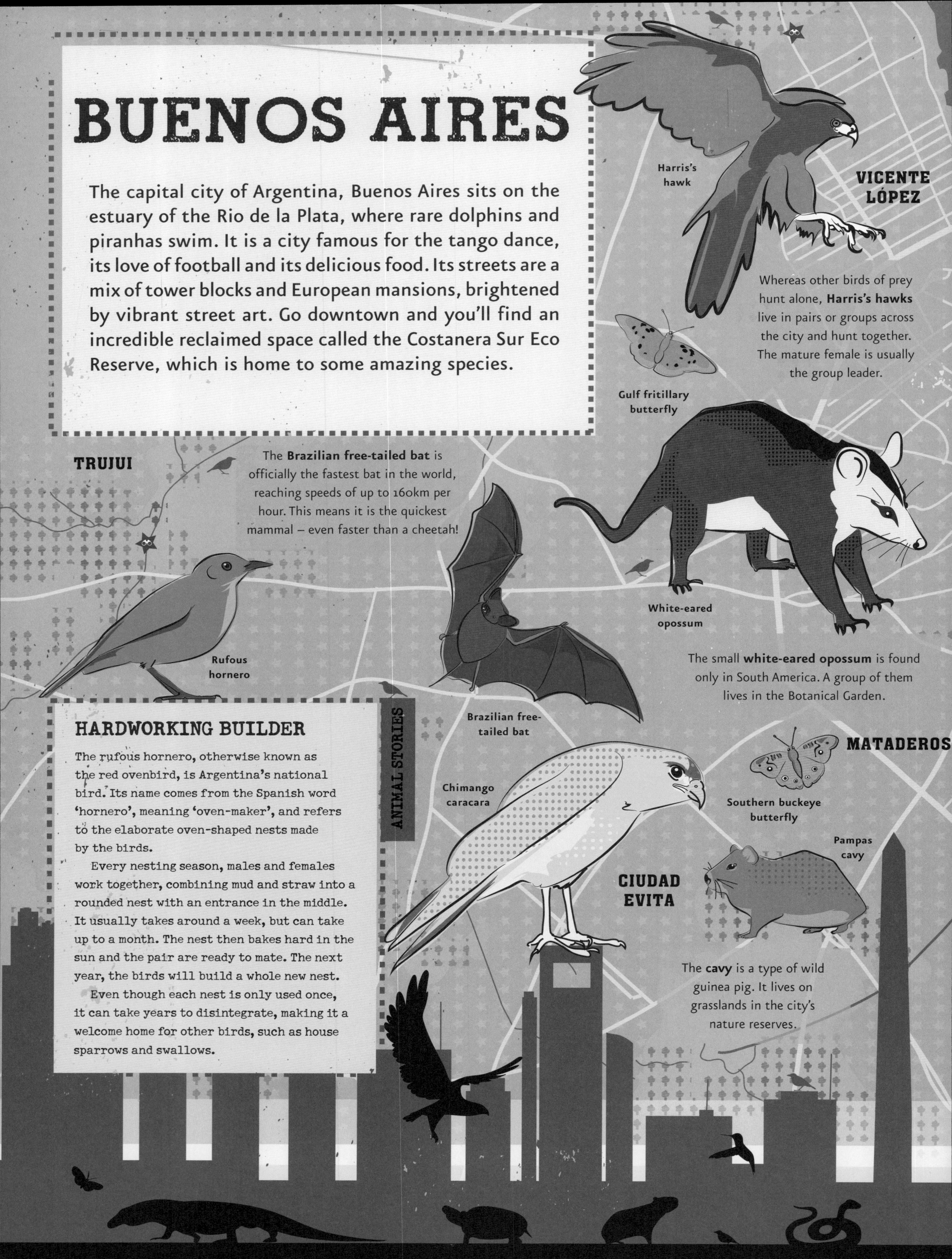

Harris's hawk

VICENTE LÓPEZ

Whereas other birds of prey hunt alone, **Harris's hawks** live in pairs or groups across the city and hunt together. The mature female is usually the group leader.

Gulf fritillary butterfly

TRUJUI

The **Brazilian free-tailed bat** is officially the fastest bat in the world, reaching speeds of up to 160km per hour. This means it is the quickest mammal – even faster than a cheetah!

White-eared opossum

Rufous hornero

The small **white-eared opossum** is found only in South America. A group of them lives in the Botanical Garden.

ANIMAL STORIES

HARDWORKING BUILDER

The rufous hornero, otherwise known as the red ovenbird, is Argentina's national bird. Its name comes from the Spanish word 'hornero', meaning 'oven-maker', and refers to the elaborate oven-shaped nests made by the birds.

Every nesting season, males and females work together, combining mud and straw into a rounded nest with an entrance in the middle. It usually takes around a week, but can take up to a month. The nest then bakes hard in the sun and the pair are ready to mate. The next year, the birds will build a whole new nest.

Even though each nest is only used once, it can take years to disintegrate, making it a welcome home for other birds, such as house sparrows and swallows.

Brazilian free-tailed bat

MATADEROS

Chimango caracara

Southern buckeye butterfly

Pampas cavy

CIUDAD EVITA

The **cavy** is a type of wild guinea pig. It lives on grasslands in the city's nature reserves.

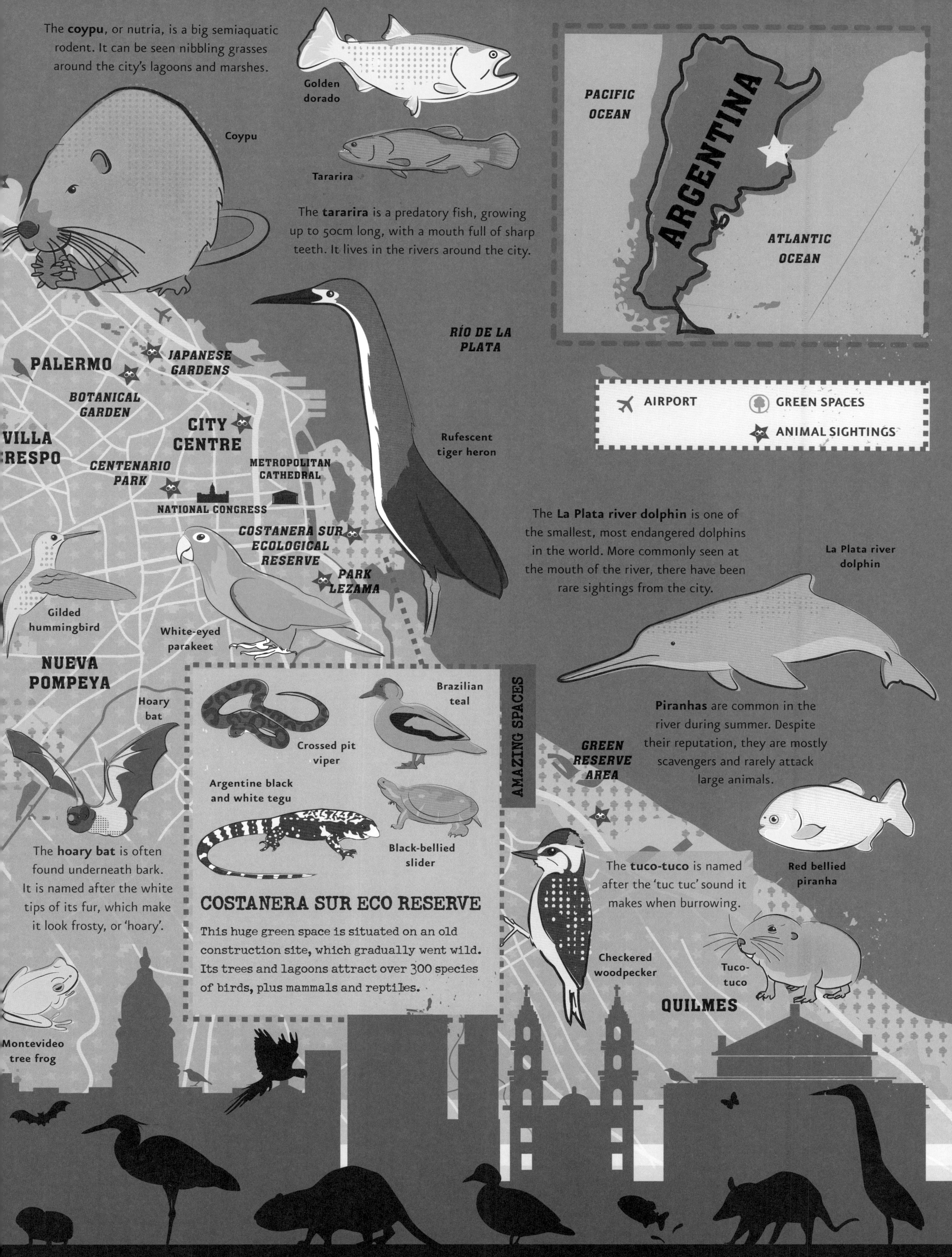

The **coypu**, or nutria, is a big semiaquatic rodent. It can be seen nibbling grasses around the city's lagoons and marshes.
Coypu
Golden dorado
Tararira
The **tararira** is a predatory fish, growing up to 50cm long, with a mouth full of sharp teeth. It lives in the rivers around the city.
PACIFIC OCEAN
ARGENTINA
ATLANTIC OCEAN
RÍO DE LA PLATA
AIRPORT
GREEN SPACES
ANIMAL SIGHTINGS
PALERMO
JAPANESE GARDENS
BOTANICAL GARDEN
CITY CENTRE
VILLA CRESPO
CENTENARIO PARK
METROPOLITAN CATHEDRAL
NATIONAL CONGRESS
COSTANERA SUR ECOLOGICAL RESERVE
PARK LEZAMA
Rufescent tiger heron
The **La Plata river dolphin** is one of the smallest, most endangered dolphins in the world. More commonly seen at the mouth of the river, there have been rare sightings from the city.
La Plata river dolphin
Gilded hummingbird
White-eyed parakeet
NUEVA POMPEYA
Hoary bat
The **hoary bat** is often found underneath bark. It is named after the white tips of its fur, which make it look frosty, or 'hoary'.
Montevideo tree frog
AMAZING SPACES
Crossed pit viper
Brazilian teal
Argentine black and white tegu
Black-bellied slider
COSTANERA SUR ECO RESERVE
This huge green space is situated on an old construction site, which gradually went wild. Its trees and lagoons attract over 300 species of birds, plus mammals and reptiles.
GREEN RESERVE AREA
Piranhas are common in the river during summer. Despite their reputation, they are mostly scavengers and rarely attack large animals.
Red bellied piranha
The **tuco-tuco** is named after the 'tuc tuc' sound it makes when burrowing.
Checkered woodpecker
Tuco-tuco
QUILMES

EUROPE

This densely populated continent has been shaped by hundreds of years of human cultivation, with much of its native forest almost completely destroyed. But from freezing winters in the north to hot summers around the Mediterranean Sea, this continent is still home to an impressive range of wildlife with plenty of surprising visitors to its towns and cities.

ICELAND
FAROE ISLANDS
NORTH ATLANTIC OCEAN
NORTH SEA
NORWAY
SWEDEN
STOCKHOLM
BALTIC SEA
DENMARK
IRELAND
UNITED KINGDOM
LONDON
NETHERLANDS
POLAND
BERLIN
KRAKOW
BELGIUM
LUXEMBOURG
GERMANY
PARIS
CZECH REPUBLIC
SLOVAKIA
LIECHTENSTEIN
AUSTRIA
FRANCE
SWITZERLAND
BUDAPEST
HUNGARY
SLOVENIA
CROATIA
SERBIA
ITALY
PORTUGAL
BOSNIA& HERZEGOVINA
ANDORRA
MONACO
SPAIN
BARCELONA
MONTENEGRO
KOSOVO
ALBANIA
ROME
MACEDONIA
MALTA
MEDITERRANEAN SEA

N
W
E
S
FINLAND
RUSSIA
ESTONIA
LATVIA
MOSCOW
LITHUANIA
BELARUS
UKRAINE
MOLDOVA
CASPIAN SEA
ROMANIA
GEORGIA
BLACK SEA
BULGARIA
TURKEY
GREECE
ATHENS
CYPRUS
EUROPE
FEATURED CITIES

LONDON

London is one of the greenest cities on the planet, with more than 40 per cent of its surface covered with parks and gardens. However, the city has not always been a haven for wildlife. Around 60 years ago, the River Thames was declared biologically dead as a result of pollution. Since then, a string of new laws has transformed the river. It now boasts over 100 species of fish, along with dolphins, porpoises, seals and even the occasional whale!

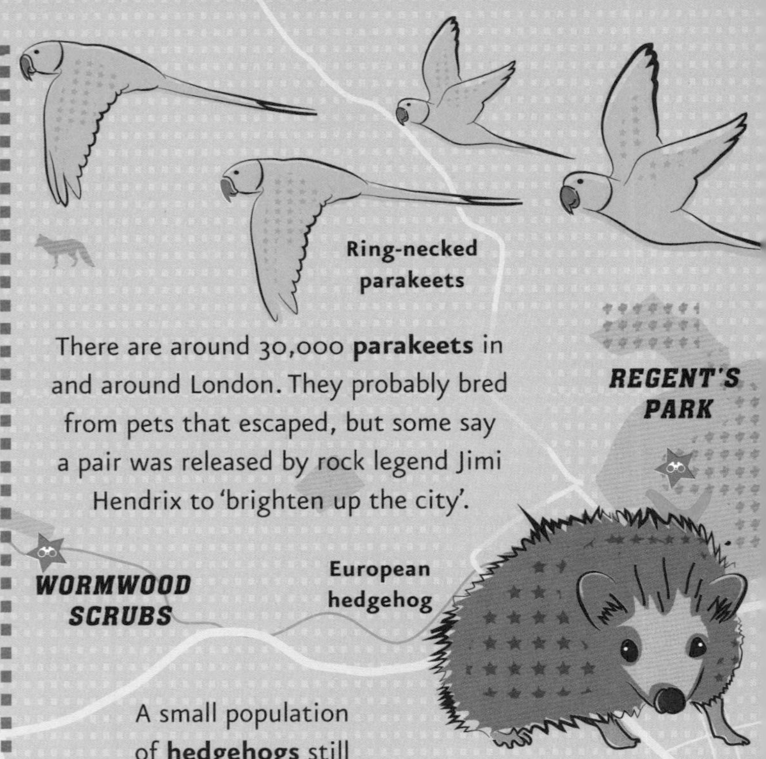

Ring-necked parakeets

There are around 30,000 **parakeets** in and around London. They probably bred from pets that escaped, but some say a pair was released by rock legend Jimi Hendrix to 'brighten up the city'.

REGENT'S PARK

WORMWOOD SCRUBS

European hedgehog

A small population of **hedgehogs** still lives and breeds in Regent's Park.

HYDE PARK

HOLLAND PARK

Red admiral butterfly

KENSINGTON

Greater flamingo

Flamingos live at the Roof Gardens on Kensington High Street!

Golden pheasant

The **golden pheasant** was introduced from China in the 1800s. A wild population still lives in Kew Gardens.

Bittern

The London Wetland Centre is a good place to see wildlife, including the **bittern**, which is one of the rarest birds in the UK. Its camouflage makes it hard to spot, so listen out for its loud 'BOOM' call.

RIVER THAMES

CHISWICK

WWT LONDON WETLAND CENTRE

BATTERSEA PARK

KEW GARDENS

Over 600 **deer** have roamed Richmond Park since 1637. See the amazing deer rut in autumn, but keep your distance as things get feisty!

Common frog

Red deer

Mute swan

Moorhen

RICHMOND PARK

EARLSFIELD

European badger

London is a hotspot for the UK's **stag beetle** population.

Stag beetle

Fallow deer

WIMBLEDON COMMON

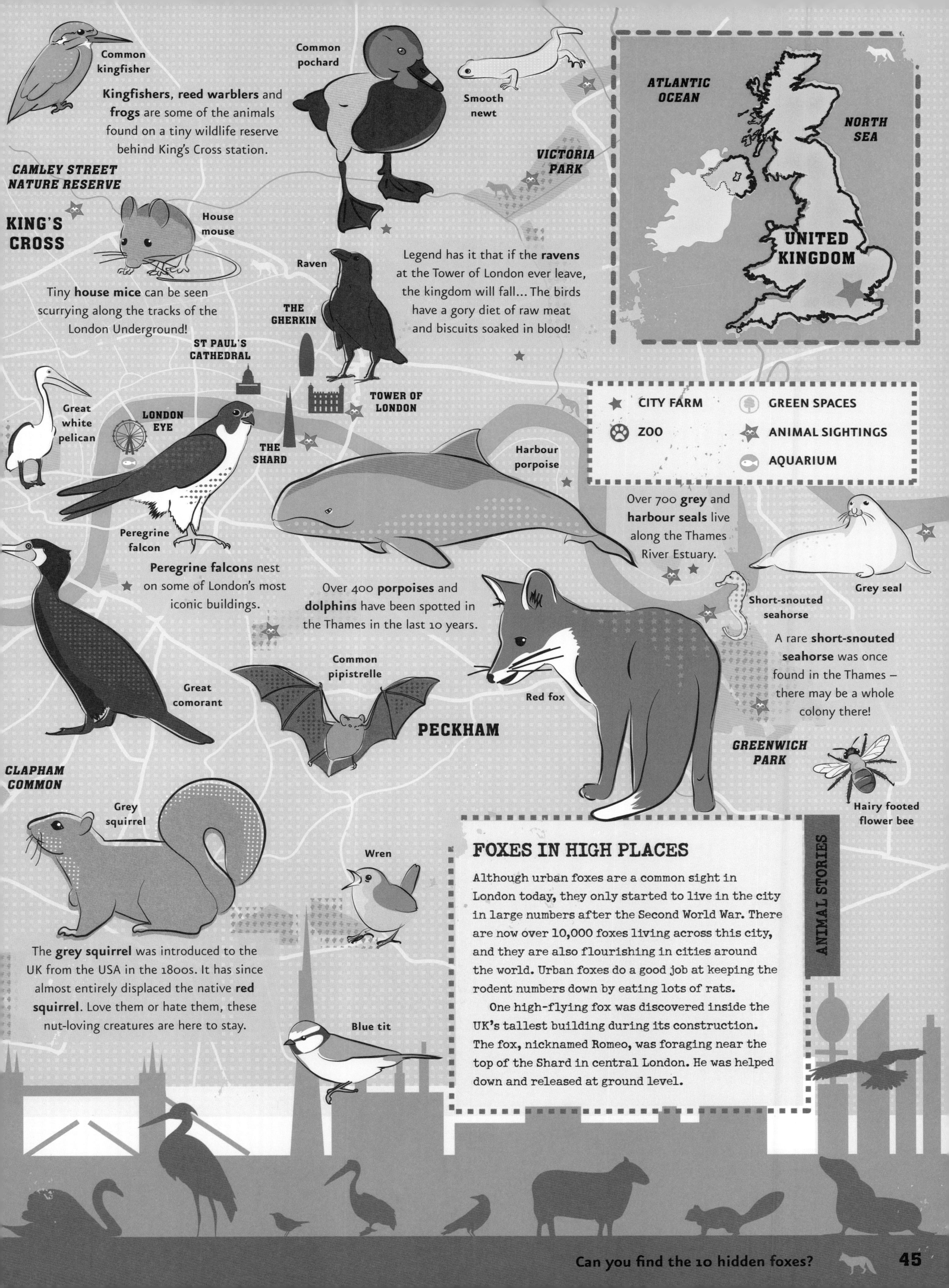

Kingfishers, **reed warblers** and **frogs** are some of the animals found on a tiny wildlife reserve behind King's Cross station.

Tiny **house mice** can be seen scurrying along the tracks of the London Underground!

Legend has it that if the **ravens** at the Tower of London ever leave, the kingdom will fall... The birds have a gory diet of raw meat and biscuits soaked in blood!

Over 700 **grey** and **harbour seals** live along the Thames River Estuary.

Peregrine falcons nest on some of London's most iconic buildings.

Over 400 **porpoises** and **dolphins** have been spotted in the Thames in the last 10 years.

A rare **short-snouted seahorse** was once found in the Thames – there may be a whole colony there!

FOXES IN HIGH PLACES

Although urban foxes are a common sight in London today, they only started to live in the city in large numbers after the Second World War. There are now over 10,000 foxes living across this city, and they are also flourishing in cities around the world. Urban foxes do a good job at keeping the rodent numbers down by eating lots of rats.

One high-flying fox was discovered inside the UK's tallest building during its construction. The fox, nicknamed Romeo, was foraging near the top of the Shard in central London. He was helped down and released at ground level.

The **grey squirrel** was introduced to the UK from the USA in the 1800s. It has since almost entirely displaced the native **red squirrel**. Love them or hate them, these nut-loving creatures are here to stay.

Can you find the 10 hidden foxes?

With world-famous art and fashion, the French capital has long been a favourite destination for visitors. Alongside monuments and galleries, you'll find parks thriving with wildlife, and flower beds as nature-friendly as they are beautiful. For the last 10 years, Paris has been pesticide free, with enormous benefits to its wildlife, in particular its bees. So look out for butterflies, birds and bees in this trend-setting green city.

Florida turtle

The invasive **Florida turtl**
originally released or escape
from captivity, can be foun
in ponds and rivers.

Paris is the urban **bee**-keeping capital of the world, with over 300 beehives in its parks, gardens, balconies and rooftops. Each hive produces around twice as much honey as a countryside hive!

Honeybee

SACR
CŒU

Grey heron

ARC DE TRIOMPHE

Herons often help themselves to fish from ponds.

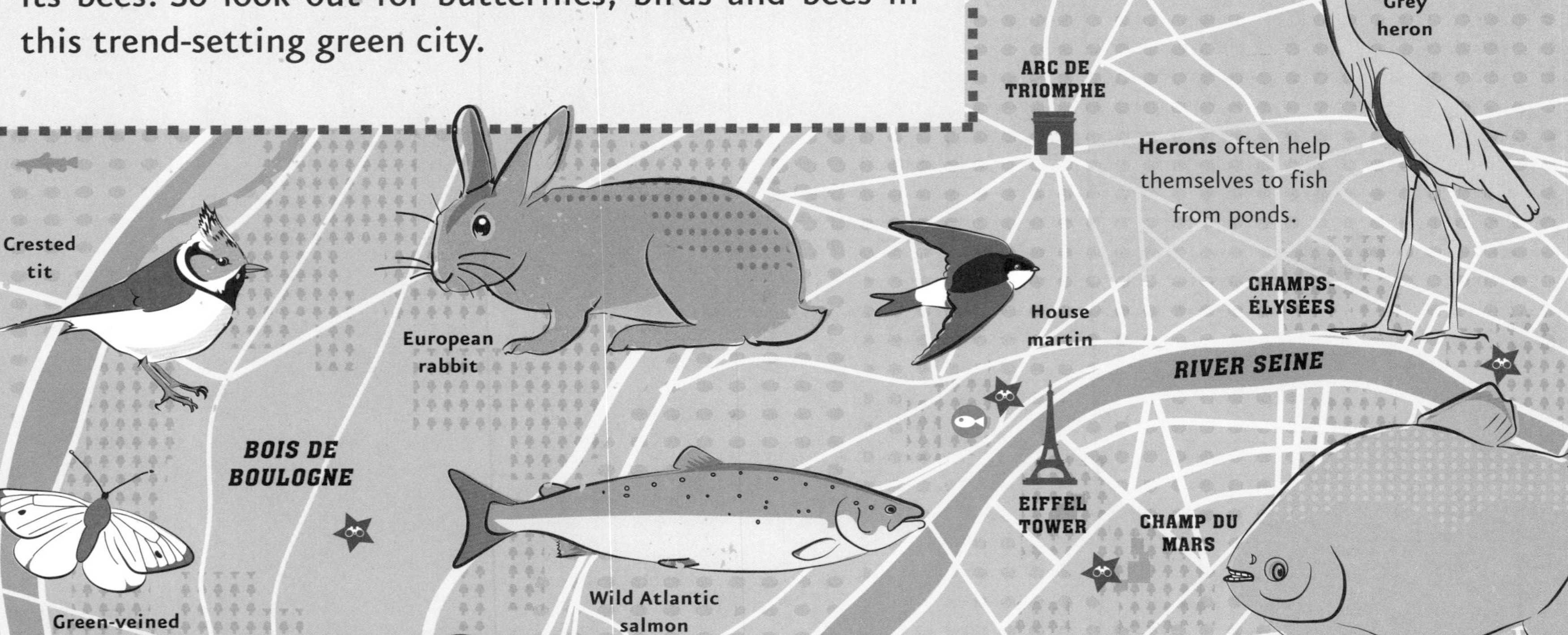

BOULOGNE-BILLANCOURT

Black-headed gull

Wild **salmon** are sometimes seen in the Seine.

The **pacu** is a South American fish, closely related to the piranha – and similarly known for its bite! One was caught in the Seine in 2013. The species has since been spotted in other European rivers.

Tawny owl

MONTPARNASSE

Little ringed plover

Little ringed plovers can be seen around water.

The **tawny owl** is seldom seen in the city centre, but can still be spotted – and heard – in the Bois de Boulogne and Bois de Vincennes.

Red fox

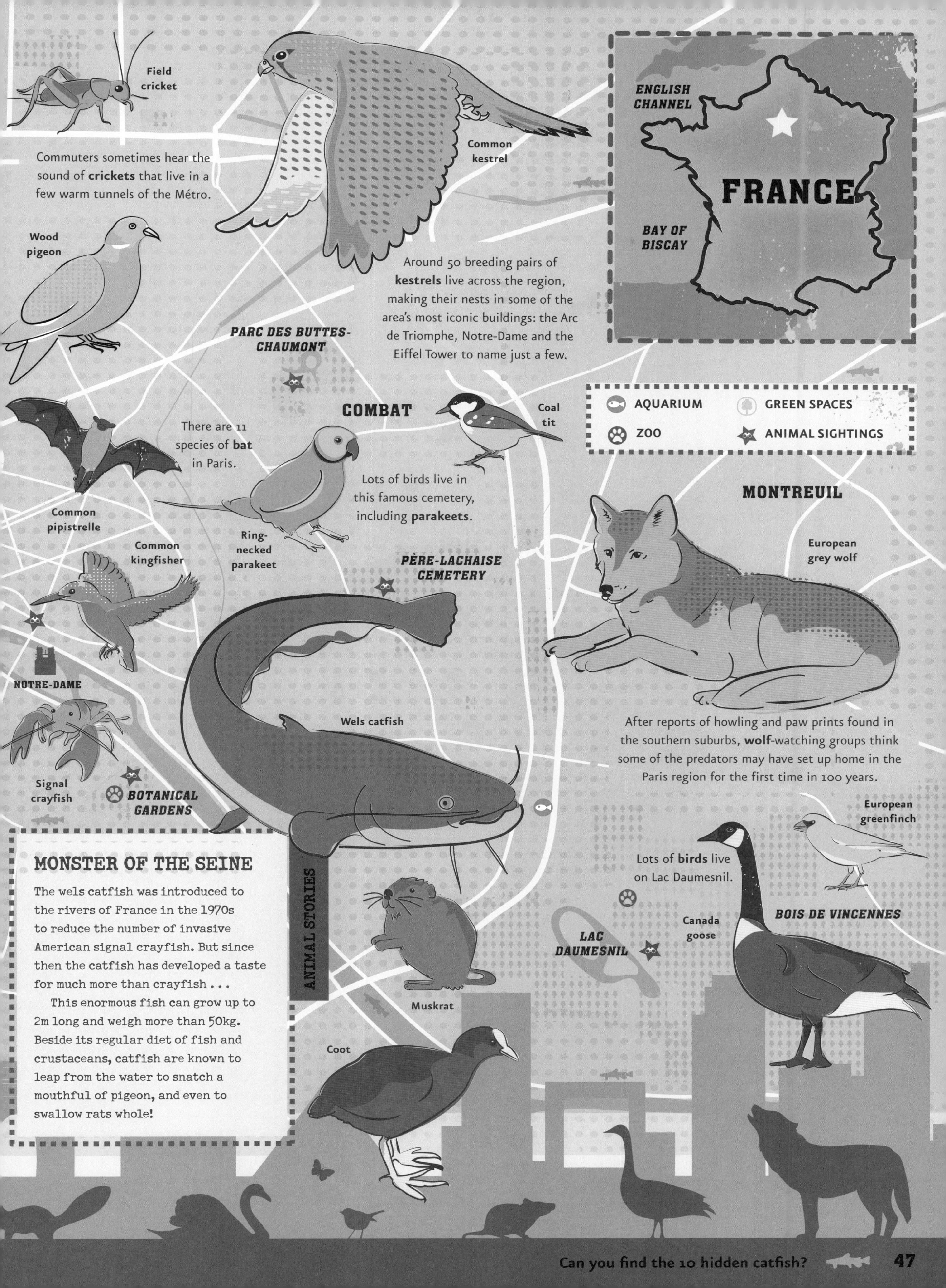
Field cricket
Commuters sometimes hear the sound of **crickets** that live in a few warm tunnels of the Métro.
Common kestrel
Wood pigeon
Around 50 breeding pairs of **kestrels** live across the region, making their nests in some of the area's most iconic buildings: the Arc de Triomphe, Notre-Dame and the Eiffel Tower to name just a few.
ENGLISH CHANNEL
FRANCE
BAY OF BISCAY
PARC DES BUTTES-CHAUMONT
COMBAT
Coal tit
AQUARIUM
GREEN SPACES
ZOO
ANIMAL SIGHTINGS
There are 11 species of **bat** in Paris.
Lots of birds live in this famous cemetery, including **parakeets**.
MONTREUIL
Common pipistrelle
Ring-necked parakeet
Common kingfisher
PÈRE-LACHAISE CEMETERY
European grey wolf
NOTRE-DAME
Wels catfish
After reports of howling and paw prints found in the southern suburbs, **wolf**-watching groups think some of the predators may have set up home in the Paris region for the first time in 100 years.
Signal crayfish
BOTANICAL GARDENS
European greenfinch
MONSTER OF THE SEINE
The wels catfish was introduced to the rivers of France in the 1970s to reduce the number of invasive American signal crayfish. But since then the catfish has developed a taste for much more than crayfish . . .
This enormous fish can grow up to 2m long and weigh more than 50kg. Beside its regular diet of fish and crustaceans, catfish are known to leap from the water to snatch a mouthful of pigeon, and even to swallow rats whole!
ANIMAL STORIES
Lots of **birds** live on Lac Daumesnil.
Canada goose
BOIS DE VINCENNES
LAC DAUMESNIL
Muskrat
Coot
Can you find the 10 hidden catfish?

BERLIN

Germany's capital is known for its bold architecture and exciting music and art scene, but is also full of green spaces. The Rivers Spree and Havel form a chain of lakes and rivers around the suburbs, making the perfect home for wildlife. There are wild boar in the parks, thousands of bats in the city centre, and a pack of wolves was even spotted just 24km out of the city in 2012 – the first wolves in the area for 100 years!

Red foxes are a common sight in Berlin. One even learned to catch the train every day. Another lives in the Chancellor's garden.

Red fox

Mandarin duck

MITTE

Little bittern

CHANCELLOR'S HOUSE

ALEXANDERPLATZ

TIERGARTEN

BRANDENBURG GATE

Eurasian beaver

1936 OLYMPIC STADIUM

A small colony of wild **herons** breeds at Berlin Zoo.

Northern goshawk

Wild boar

Grey heron

TEMPELHOF FELD

A platform on the steep-sided river provides a resting place for **beavers** as they travel through the city.

There are 120 pairs of **goshawks** in the city, one of the highest densities in Europe. A good spot to see them is the Tempelhofer Feld and the Tiergarten.

Blackcap

RIVER HAVEL

GRUNEWALD FOREST

BOTANICAL GARDEN

Wild boar roam the city's green areas. They are mostly active at night, but sometimes wander onto the streets and disrupt traffic.

MARIENDORF

Found all over the city, **martens** sometimes sleep in car engines and occasionally even chew through the wiring!

European hedgehog

Beech marten

Common swifts
There are three pairs of **white-tailed eagles** breeding in Berlin.
White-tailed eagle
NORTH SEA
BALTIC SEA
GERMANY
LICHTENBERG
Berlin has thousands of **swifts** – they spend their whole lives flying, only landing to breed.
Common raccoon
STRIPY BANDITS
Originally from America, raccoons were brought over to Germany in the 1930s and bred for their fur. The story goes that some escaped from a fur farm near Berlin at the end of the Second World War. They quickly multiplied and there are now over 600 raccoons in the city! In 2008, one moved into the garage of a luxury hotel in Alexanderplatz. The raccoon, nicknamed Alex, lived there for almost a year before moving on.
ANIMAL STORIES
CITY FARM
GREEN SPACES
ZOO
ANIMAL SIGHTINGS
Red squirrels can be seen in parks and gardens across the city, and there is even a squirrel bridge over the Müggelseedamm, to help the squirrels get from one side of the road to the other.
GÖRLITZER PARK
See **reed warblers** in reeds and bushes along the riverbank.
Brambling
Red squirrel
TREPTOWER PARK
RIVER SPREE
Sand lizard
European rabbit
Reed warbler
Great crested grebe
The biggest lake in Berlin is home to **divers** and **grebes**.
Eurasian robin
MÜGGELSEEDAMM
MÜGGELSEE
European grey wolf
Great northern diver
Common pipistrelle
4,500 **bats** spend the winter in Berlin, living in 35 different colonies.
Can you find the 10 hidden boars?

ATHENS

Athens is a densely populated area, packed with street markets and cafes, and overlooked by the ancient ruins of the Acropolis. But it is also full of creatures. Listen for the chatter of goldfinches over the hustle and bustle; look for tortoises and turtles sunbathing on top of each other at the National Garden; and keep your eyes open for owls, hoopoes and kestrels high on Lycabettus Hill, where you'll find over 65 species of bird.

In Greek mythology, Athena, the goddess of wisdom, is often accompanied by a **little owl**. You can still see the owls – which really are little – on Acropolis Hill, even in the daytime!

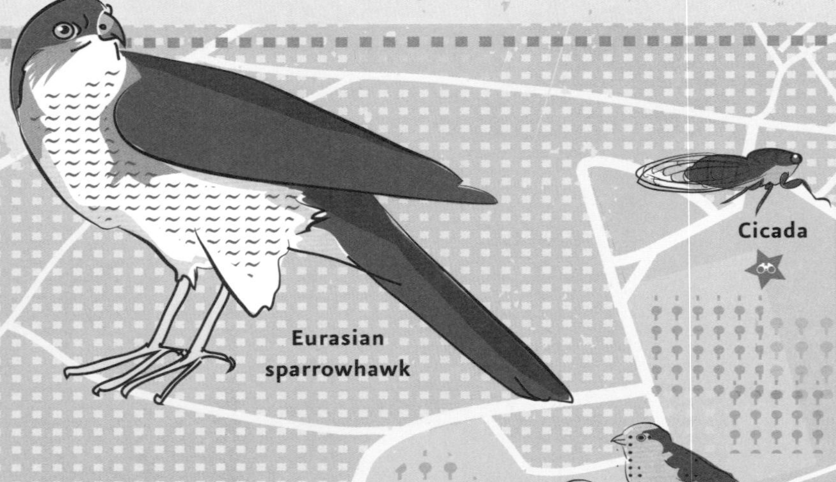

Lots of **swallows** and **house martins** swoop over the capital, eating insects in great numbers.

A charity called 'Nine Lives' helps Athens' many **stray cats** by feeding, treating and neutering them, or by finding them homes.

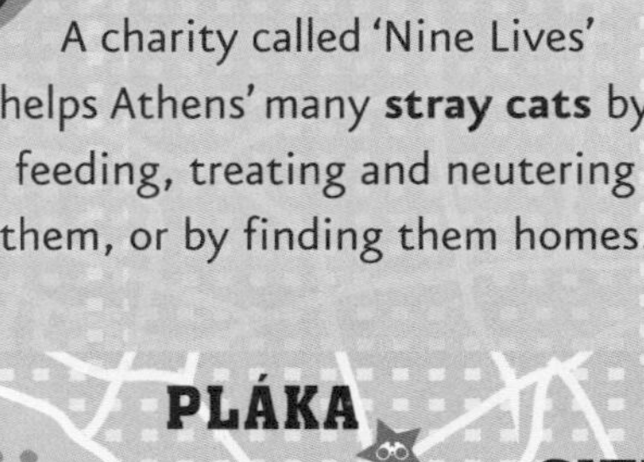

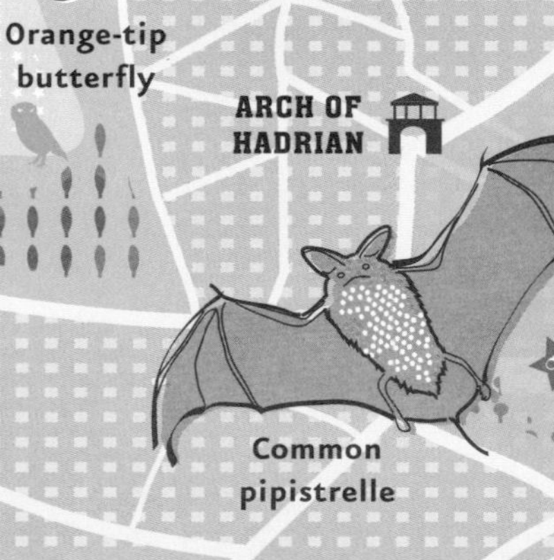

Hedgehogs live on Philopappou Hill.

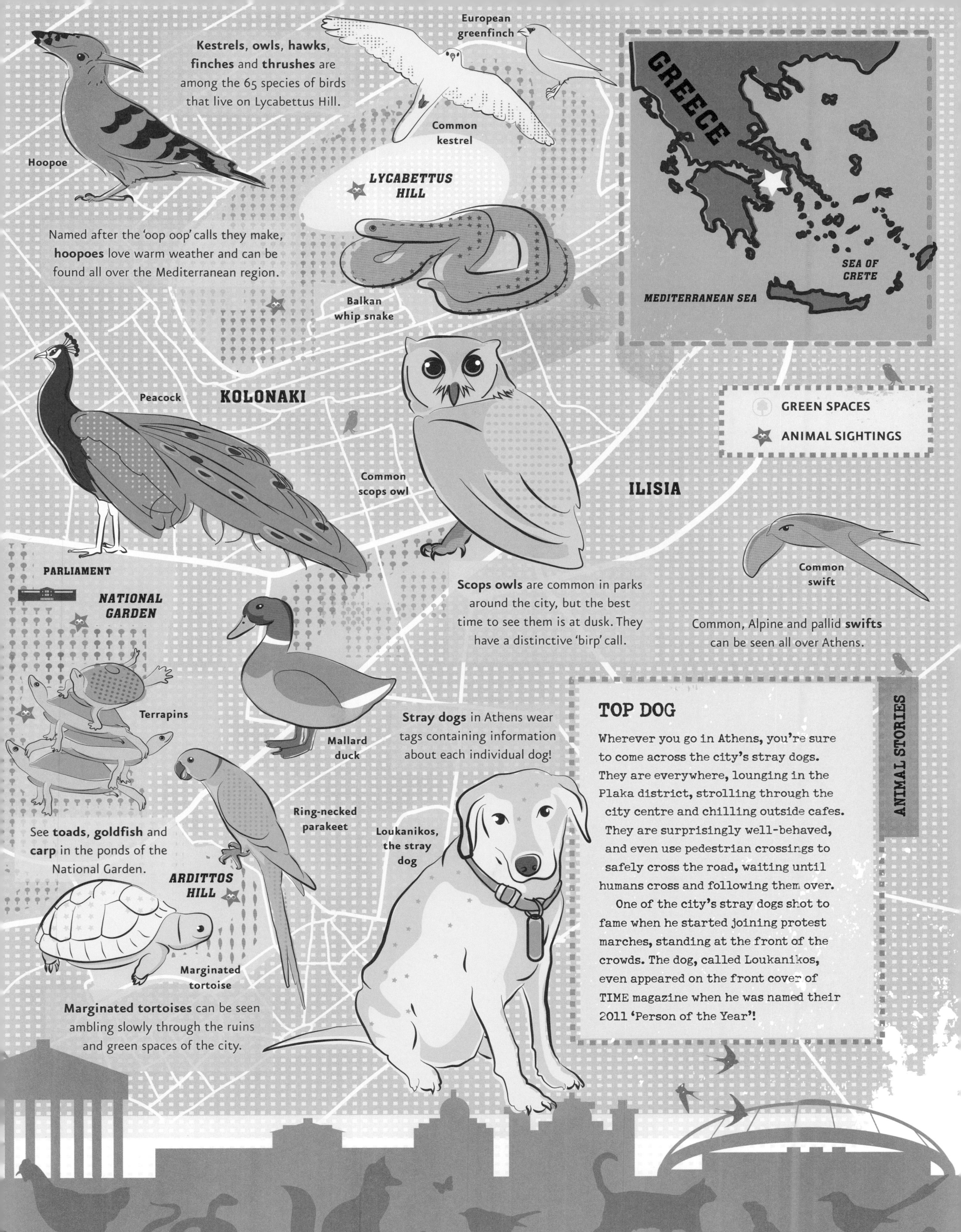

ANIMAL STORIES

TOP DOG

Wherever you go in Athens, you're sure to come across the city's stray dogs. They are everywhere, lounging in the Plaka district, strolling through the city centre and chilling outside cafes. They are surprisingly well-behaved, and even use pedestrian crossings to safely cross the road, waiting until humans cross and following them over.

One of the city's stray dogs shot to fame when he started joining protest marches, standing at the front of the crowds. The dog, called Loukanikos, even appeared on the front cover of TIME magazine when he was named their 2011 'Person of the Year'!

Can you find the 10 hidden owls?

STOCKHOLM

The capital of Sweden sits across 14 islands, connected by 57 bridges. Cobblestone streets wind through the old town, while the newer districts feature dramatic, cutting-edge buildings fringed by green spaces. Summer days are long and lazy, while Swedish winters are dark and cold, with snow on the ground and ice on the water – a perfect time to feed the birds at Kungsträdgården and Rålambshovsparken!

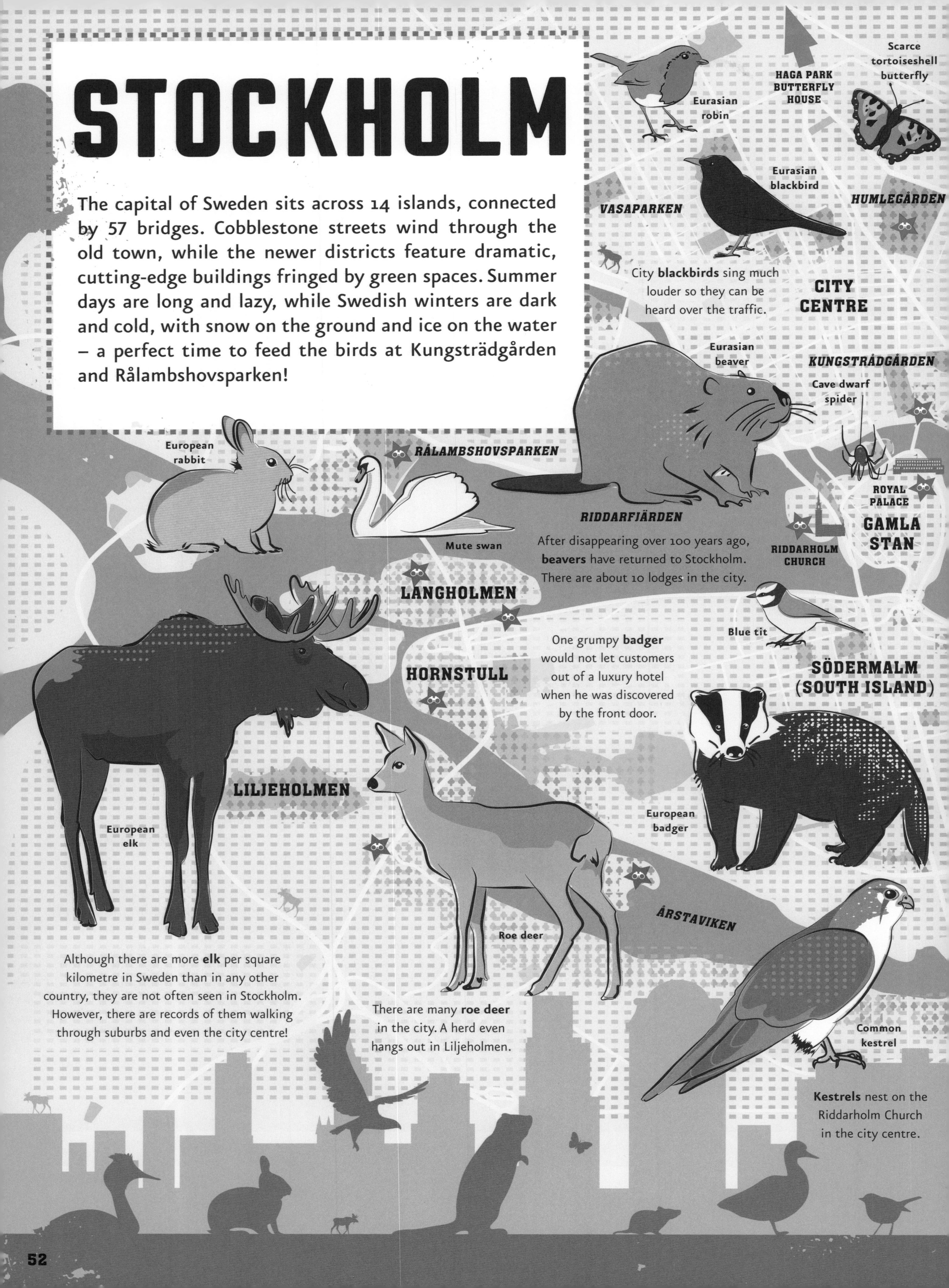

City **blackbirds** sing much louder so they can be heard over the traffic.

After disappearing over 100 years ago, **beavers** have returned to Stockholm. There are about 10 lodges in the city.

One grumpy **badger** would not let customers out of a luxury hotel when he was discovered by the front door.

Although there are more **elk** per square kilometre in Sweden than in any other country, they are not often seen in Stockholm. However, there are records of them walking through suburbs and even the city centre!

There are many **roe deer** in the city. A herd even hangs out in Liljeholmen.

Kestrels nest on the Riddarholm Church in the city centre.

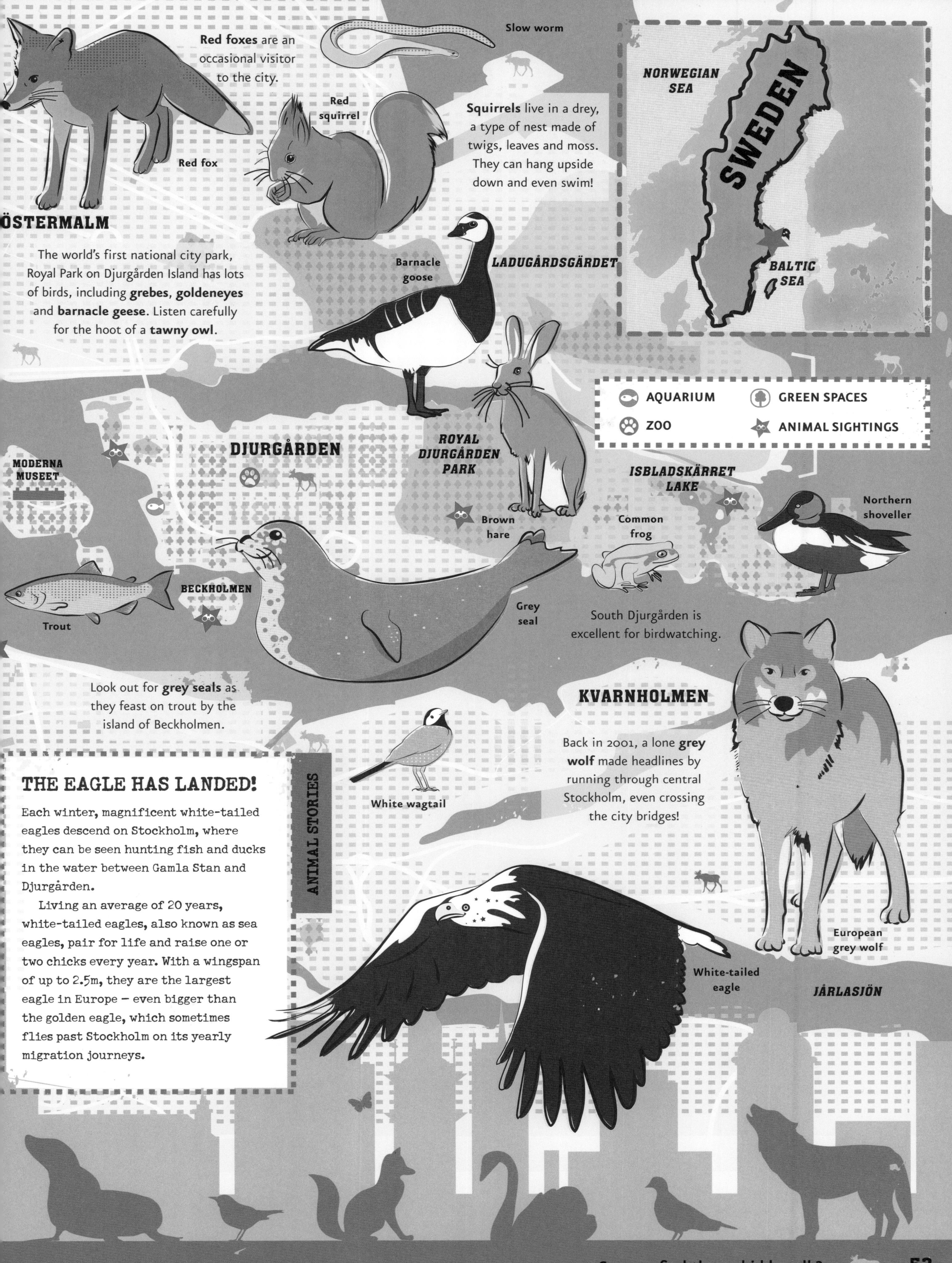

Red foxes are an occasional visitor to the city.
Slow worm
Red squirrel
Red fox
Squirrels live in a drey, a type of nest made of twigs, leaves and moss. They can hang upside down and even swim!
NORWEGIAN SEA
SWEDEN
BALTIC SEA
ÖSTERMALM
The world's first national city park, Royal Park on Djurgården Island has lots of birds, including grebes, goldeneyes and barnacle geese. Listen carefully for the hoot of a tawny owl.
Barnacle goose
LADUGÅRDSGÄRDET
AQUARIUM
GREEN SPACES
ZOO
ANIMAL SIGHTINGS
MODERNA MUSEET
DJURGÅRDEN
ROYAL DJURGÅRDEN PARK
ISBLADSKÄRRET LAKE
Northern shoveller
Brown hare
Common frog
BECKHOLMEN
Trout
Grey seal
South Djurgården is excellent for birdwatching.
Look out for grey seals as they feast on trout by the island of Beckholmen.
KVARNHOLMEN
Back in 2001, a lone grey wolf made headlines by running through central Stockholm, even crossing the city bridges!
THE EAGLE HAS LANDED!
ANIMAL STORIES
Each winter, magnificent white-tailed eagles descend on Stockholm, where they can be seen hunting fish and ducks in the water between Gamla Stan and Djurgården.
Living an average of 20 years, white-tailed eagles, also known as sea eagles, pair for life and raise one or two chicks every year. With a wingspan of up to 2.5m, they are the largest eagle in Europe – even bigger than the golden eagle, which sometimes flies past Stockholm on its yearly migration journeys.
White wagtail
European grey wolf
White-tailed eagle
JÅRLASJÖN

MOSCOW

Sitting on the River Moskva, Moscow is Russia's capital and largest city. At its centre is the Kremlin, a towering medieval fortress that is the official residence of Russia's president. Just a short drive away you'll find one of the largest city forests in the world: Losiny Ostrov ('Elk Island' in Russian) National Park. Moscow's urban areas are also a refuge for wintering waterfowl, with a citizen bird count every year to check their numbers.

AMAZING SPACES

Black woodpecker

Quail

Wild boar

Roe deer

Eurasian beaver

LOSINY OSTROV NATIONAL PARK

Once the hunting ground of tsars, this reserve covers 116sq km. It has more than 200 species, including otters, deer, weasels, owls and many amphibians, including northern crested newts.

Common across Europe, the **short-toed treecreeper** runs up and down tree trunks looking for insects and spiders to eat.

Red squirrels, which live in parks across the city, are a favourite with locals.

Moscow's **ruddy shelducks** are thought to have escaped from Moscow Zoo in the 1950s and adapted to life in the city habitat.

Gorky Park is full of wintering **ducks** and **pigeons**.

MOSCOW'S 'METRO DOGS'

Moscow's underground system is one of the oldest and largest in the world. And surprisingly it's even used by a small group of the city's stray dogs. These street-savvy commuter dogs use the metro to travel from place to place. They know where to get on and off the trains, and have a knack for finding people who will offer them food, while avoiding other less friendly passengers.

This amazing behaviour suggests that dogs are evolving alongside humans, and learning from our behaviour. It also shows an impressive ability to survive in a growing urban environment.

KRAKOW

One of the oldest cities in Poland, Krakow sits on the River Vistula in the south of the country. Supposedly built over the cave of a great dragon, the city is a maze of medieval buildings and narrow, winding streets. With 40 parks and five nature reserves, Krakow also has a diverse range of wildlife to be seen in and around the city. Incredible sightings include wandering wild boar and seven species of woodpecker.

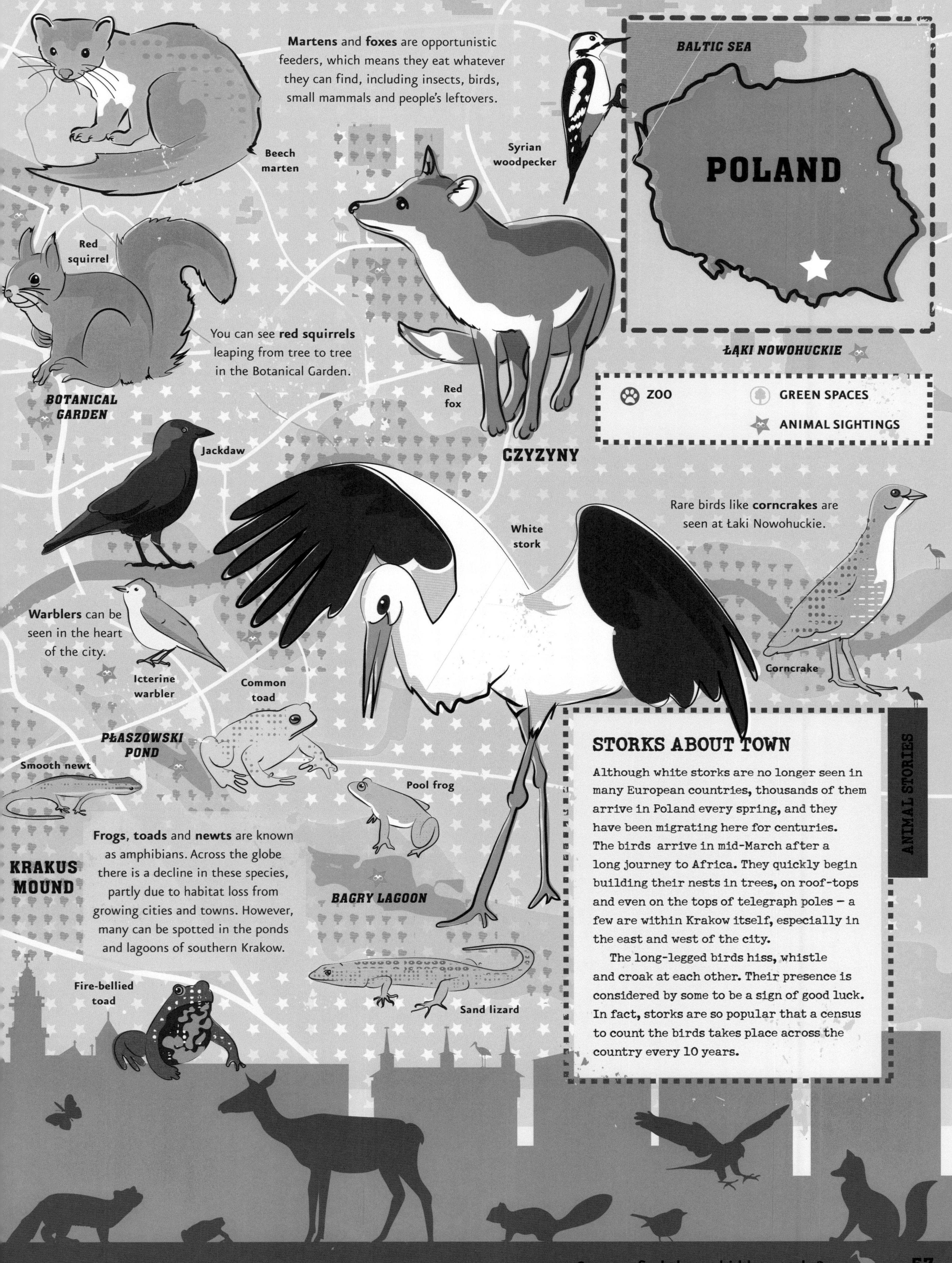

STORKS ABOUT TOWN

Although white storks are no longer seen in many European countries, thousands of them arrive in Poland every spring, and they have been migrating here for centuries. The birds arrive in mid-March after a long journey to Africa. They quickly begin building their nests in trees, on roof-tops and even on the tops of telegraph poles – a few are within Krakow itself, especially in the east and west of the city.

The long-legged birds hiss, whistle and croak at each other. Their presence is considered by some to be a sign of good luck. In fact, storks are so popular that a census to count the birds takes place across the country every 10 years.

Can you find the 10 hidden storks?

BUDAPEST

Hungary's capital, Budapest, is considered to be one of the most beautiful cities in Europe. The city is in two halves, with Buda and Pest divided by the River Danube. Budapest is best known for its elegant architecture and historic bath houses, fed by over 100 thermal springs. Its green spaces, waterways and suburbs provide a diverse range of habitats and wildlife corridors (green areas that link together habitats dotted through a city).

Smooth newt

Red squirrel

JAPANESE GARDEN

MARGARET ISLAND

Margaret Island is home to **red squirrels**, **ducks**, **hedgehogs** and **nightingales**.

CITY PARK

Wild boar often come into the city. A few even have the strange habit of jumping into the River Danube in the Buda (west) side of the city and swimming over to the Pest (east) side.

The Budapest region boasts seven woodpecker species, including the **middle spotted**, **black** and **greyheaded woodpeckers** of the Buda Hills as well as the more urban **Syrian woodpecker**.

The **common vole** is prey to city **kestrels** and **barn owls**.

Named by the Romans, the **edible dormouse** is found in urban attics and parks. These big-eyed, fluffy-tailed rodents are excellent climbers.

The **green toad** likes to hang out under street lights across the city.

There are 16 species of reptiles in Budapest, including the **green lizard**, found all over the city.

MARTENS IN THE MIDDLE

ANIMAL STORIES

Beech martens are small, weasel-like mammals that have colonised many cities and towns across Europe. They eat a wide range of food, including insects, fruit, small mammals and rubbish.

In Budapest, beech martens live in attics, sheds and gardens, where they have good access to food and shelter. One marten family even took up residence in the attic of the Vatican Embassy in Budapest!

ROME

The capital of Italy dates back nearly 3,000 years and is bursting with history, from the Colosseum where gladiators once fought, to Michelangelo's paintings in the Vatican's Sistine Chapel. Lizards sunbathe amid ancient ruins, while birds and bats swoop above magnificent piazzas. In fact, Rome's starlings are so numerous that their droppings can cause a real problem – whole roads sometimes have to be shut while their slippery mess is cleaned up!

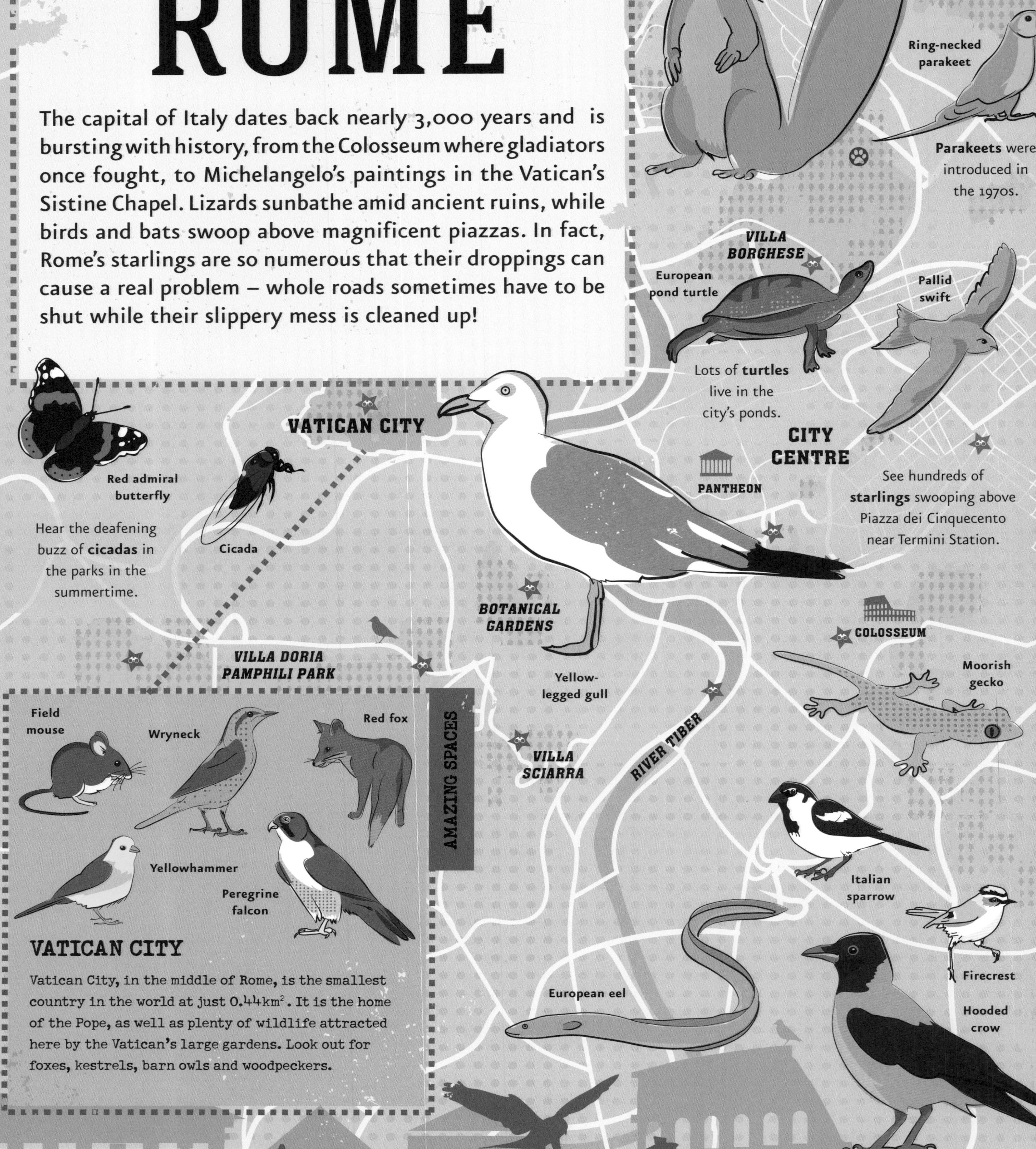

VATICAN CITY

Vatican City, in the middle of Rome, is the smallest country in the world at just 0.44km². It is the home of the Pope, as well as plenty of wildlife attracted here by the Vatican's large gardens. Look out for foxes, kestrels, barn owls and woodpeckers.

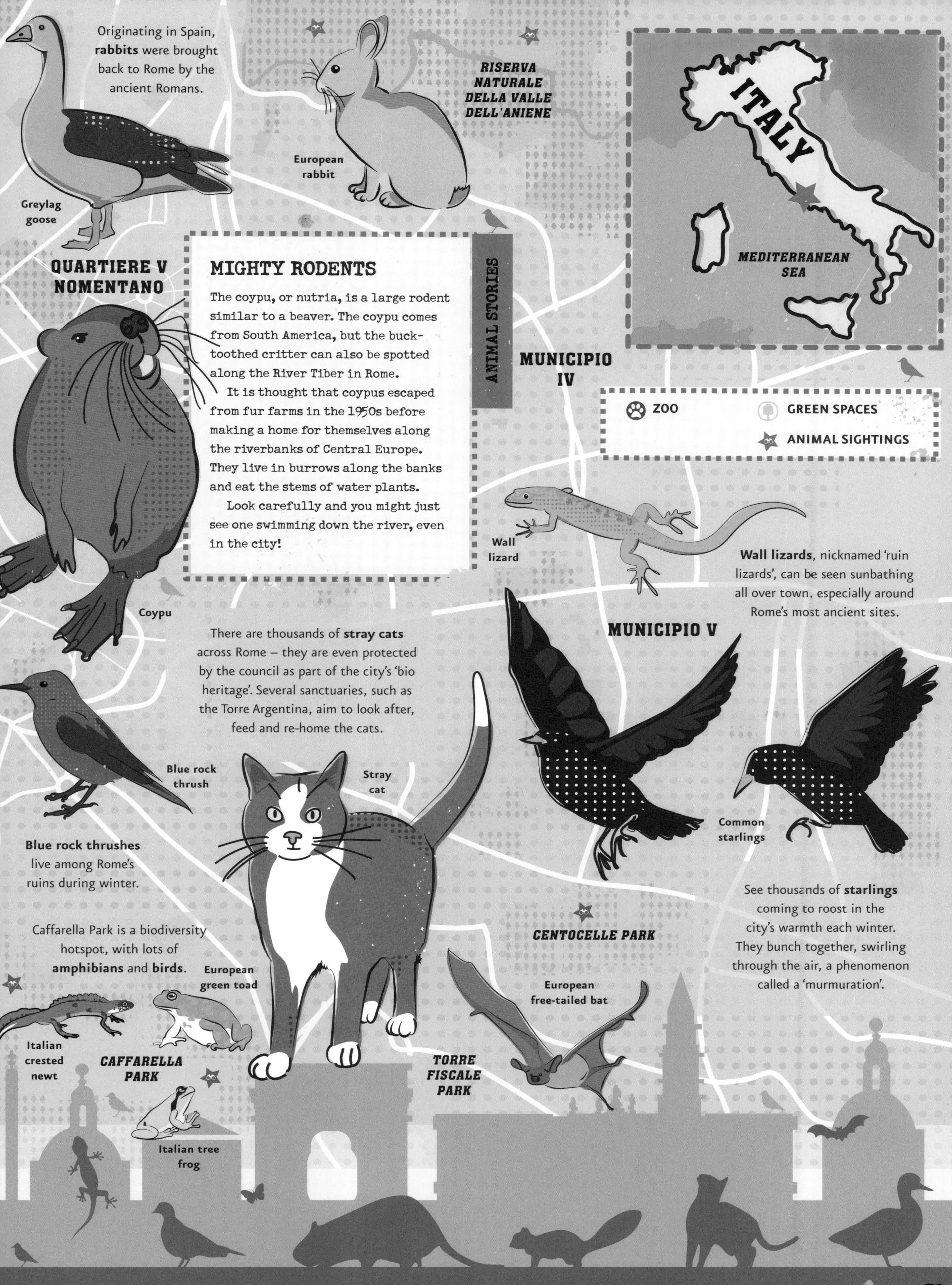

Originating in Spain, rabbits were brought back to Rome by the ancient Romans.
Greylag goose
European rabbit
RISERVA NATURALE DELLA VALLE DELL'ANIENE
ITALY
MEDITERRANEAN SEA
QUARTIERE V NOMENTANO
ANIMAL STORIES
MIGHTY RODENTS
The coypu, or nutria, is a large rodent similar to a beaver. The coypu comes from South America, but the buck-toothed critter can also be spotted along the River Tiber in Rome.
It is thought that coypus escaped from fur farms in the 1950s before making a home for themselves along the riverbanks of Central Europe. They live in burrows along the banks and eat the stems of water plants.
Look carefully and you might just see one swimming down the river, even in the city!
MUNICIPIO IV
ZOO
GREEN SPACES
ANIMAL SIGHTINGS
Wall lizard
Wall lizards, nicknamed 'ruin lizards', can be seen sunbathing all over town, especially around Rome's most ancient sites.
Coypu
There are thousands of stray cats across Rome – they are even protected by the council as part of the city's 'bio heritage'. Several sanctuaries, such as the Torre Argentina, aim to look after, feed and re-home the cats.
MUNICIPIO V
Blue rock thrush
Stray cat
Common starlings
Blue rock thrushes live among Rome's ruins during winter.
See thousands of starlings coming to roost in the city's warmth each winter. They bunch together, swirling through the air, a phenomenon called a 'murmuration'.
Caffarella Park is a biodiversity hotspot, with lots of amphibians and birds.
European green toad
CENTOCELLE PARK
European free-tailed bat
Italian crested newt
CAFFARELLA PARK
TORRE FISCALE PARK
Italian tree frog
Can you find the 10 hidden starlings?

BARCELONA

The capital of the Catalan region of Spain, Barcelona lies on the Mediterranean coast. Its streets boast an amazing array of brightly coloured, strangely shaped buildings by the famous architect Antoni Gaudi. The city also has a diverse bird population, from peregrine falcons and kestrels in its centre to herons and ibis flying through the skies towards the marshes of the Delta de Llobregat.

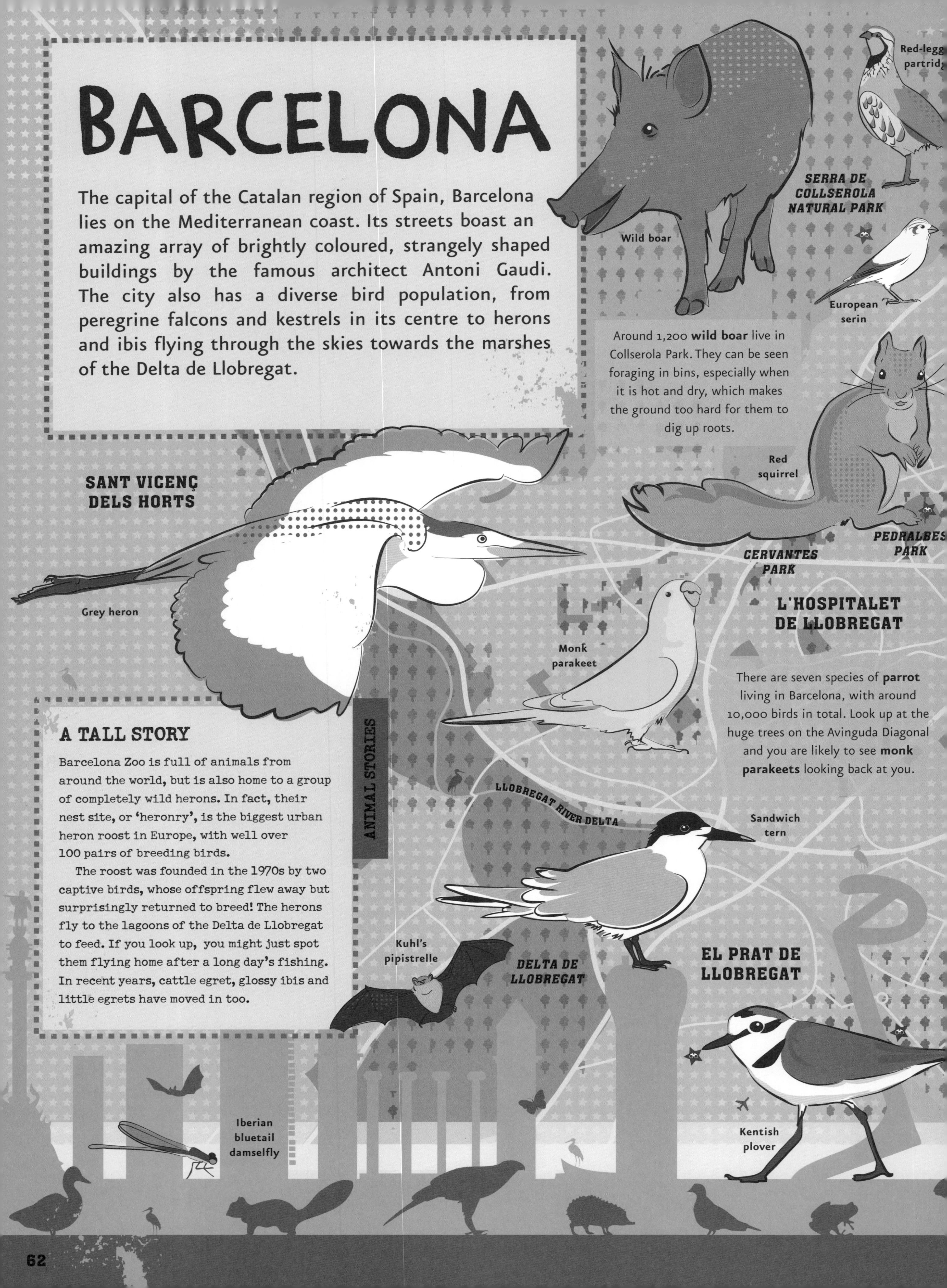

Around 1,200 **wild boar** live in Collserola Park. They can be seen foraging in bins, especially when it is hot and dry, which makes the ground too hard for them to dig up roots.

There are seven species of **parrot** living in Barcelona, with around 10,000 birds in total. Look up at the huge trees on the Avinguda Diagonal and you are likely to see **monk parakeets** looking back at you.

ANIMAL STORIES

A TALL STORY

Barcelona Zoo is full of animals from around the world, but is also home to a group of completely wild herons. In fact, their nest site, or 'heronry', is the biggest urban heron roost in Europe, with well over 100 pairs of breeding birds.

The roost was founded in the 1970s by two captive birds, whose offspring flew away but surprisingly returned to breed! The herons fly to the lagoons of the Delta de Llobregat to feed. If you look up, you might just spot them flying home after a long day's fishing. In recent years, cattle egret, glossy ibis and little egrets have moved in too.

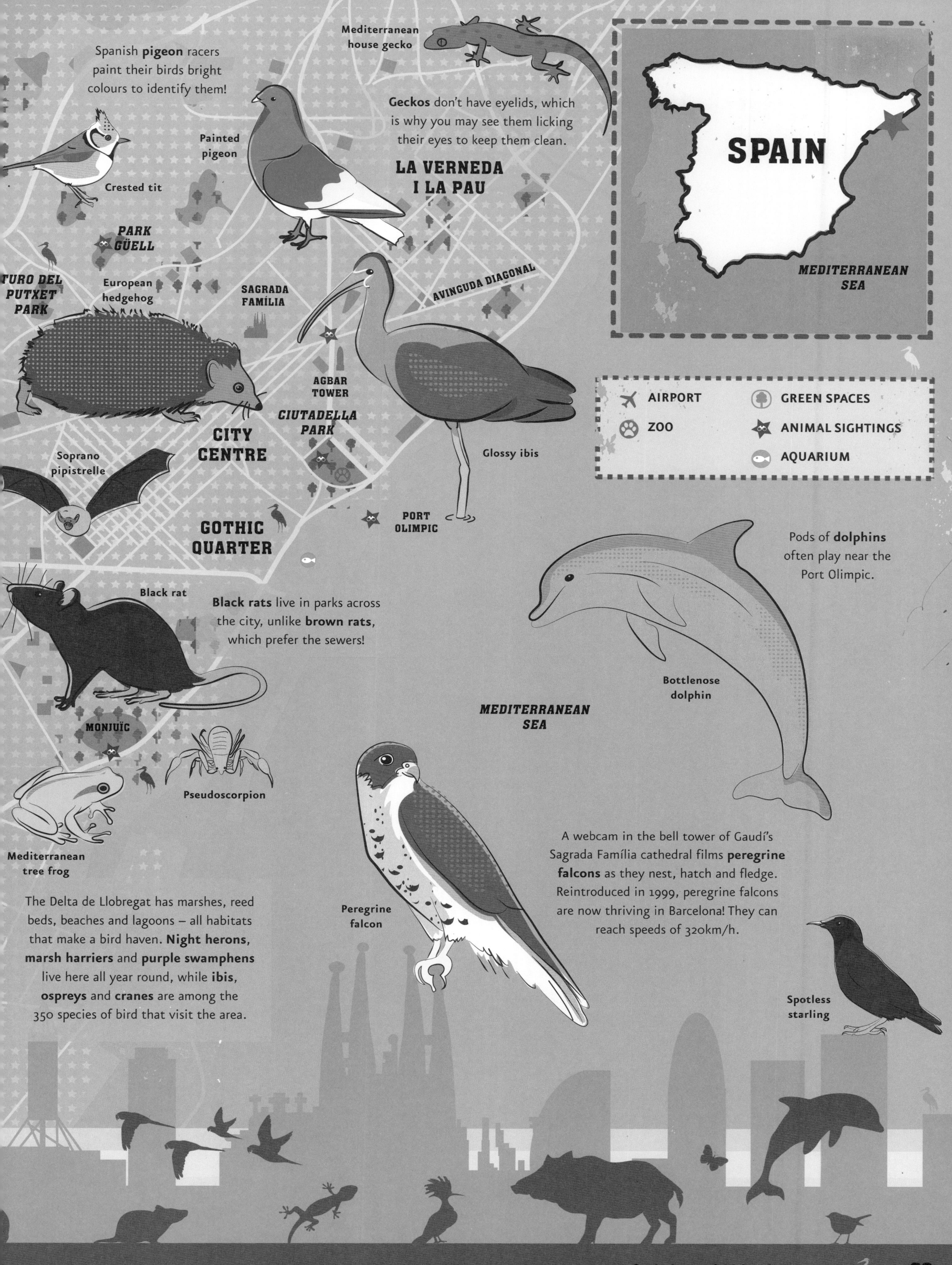

Can you find the 10 hidden herons?

AFRICA

Africa has a hot climate with habitats from deserts to rainforests. Many of its cities are relatively new and growing at incredible rates, bringing more animals into an urban setting, and creating challenges for wildlife and humans alike. With Africa boasting some of the most iconic animals in the world, such as lions and elephants, even the cities here are known for their safari sightings!

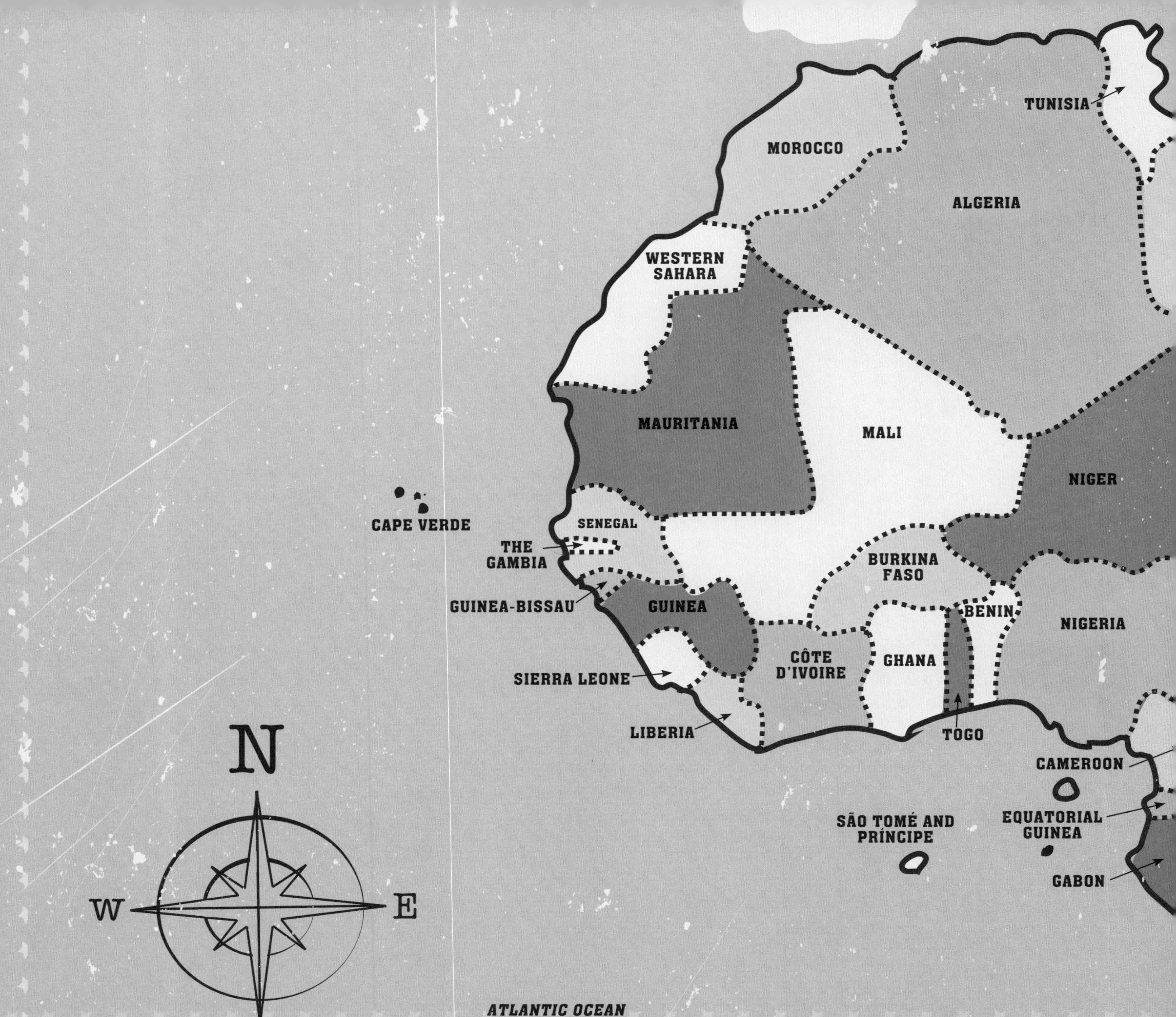

AFRICA

 **FEATURED CITIES**

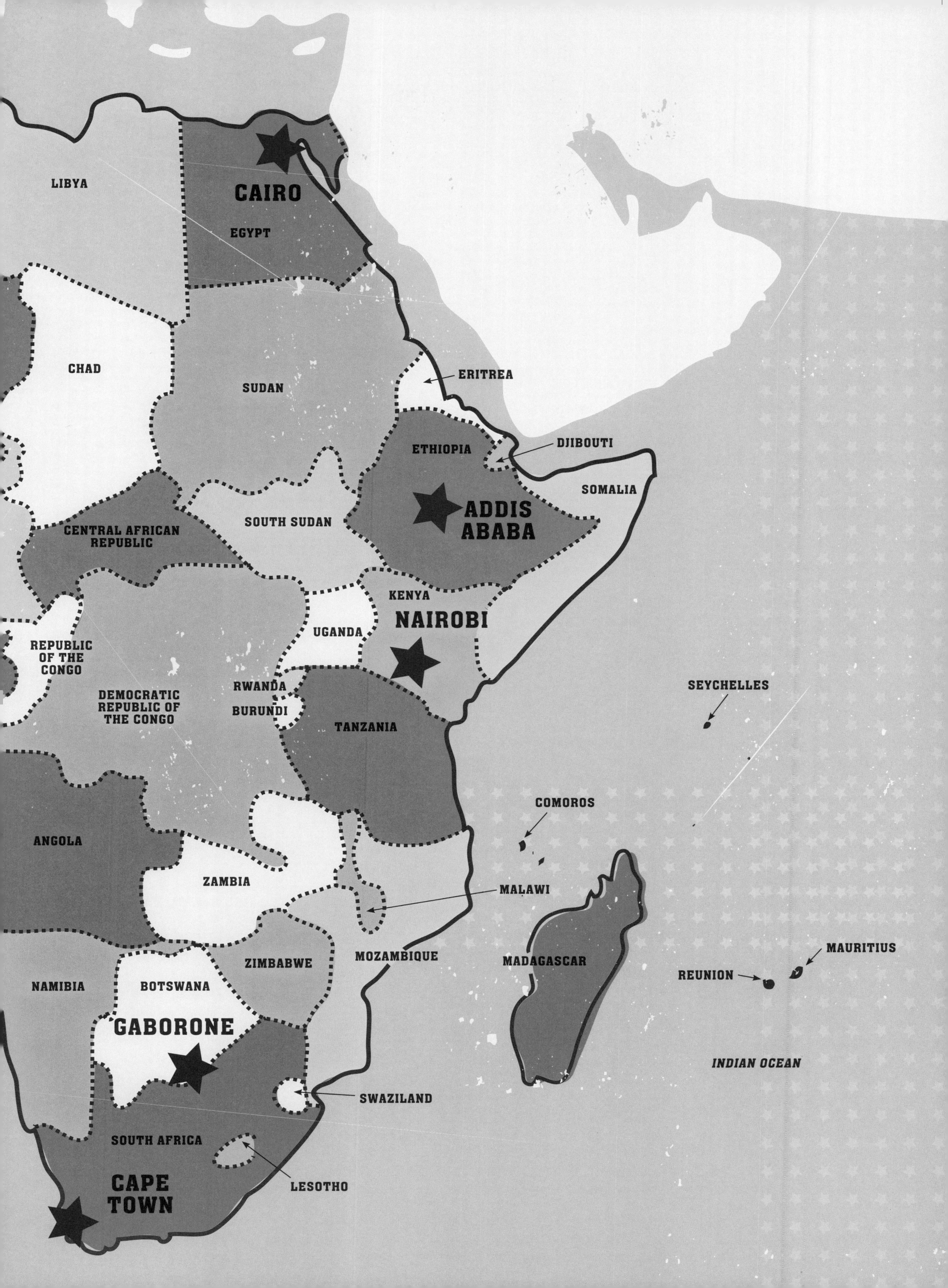
LIBYA
CAIRO
EGYPT
CHAD
SUDAN
ERITREA
ETHIOPIA
DJIBOUTI
SOMALIA
ADDIS ABABA
SOUTH SUDAN
CENTRAL AFRICAN REPUBLIC
KENYA
NAIROBI
UGANDA
REPUBLIC OF THE CONGO
DEMOCRATIC REPUBLIC OF THE CONGO
RWANDA
BURUNDI
TANZANIA
SEYCHELLES
COMOROS
ANGOLA
ZAMBIA
MALAWI
MOZAMBIQUE
MADAGASCAR
ZIMBABWE
MAURITIUS
REUNION
NAMIBIA
BOTSWANA
GABORONE
INDIAN OCEAN
SWAZILAND
SOUTH AFRICA
LESOTHO
CAPE TOWN

CAIRO

The capital of Egypt is an ancient city, in a region that goes back to the time of the pharaohs. The longest river in the world, the Nile, flows through Cairo, supporting the region's agriculture and its natural habitats, and the nearby city of Giza is the site of the pyramids, the last surviving Wonder of the Ancient World. Despite the challenges of urban life, animals still manage to live side-by-side with people in this sprawling urban landscape.

Cobras can sometimes be found around canals and inside old buildings!

Egrets and **herons** fish in the city's rivers and canals.

The **thick-knee** is commonly heard but rarely seen.

Dromedaries or **Arabian camels** have fat stores in their hump which break down into water and energy, so they can go for days without water. There are no wild dromedaries as they are all domesticated.

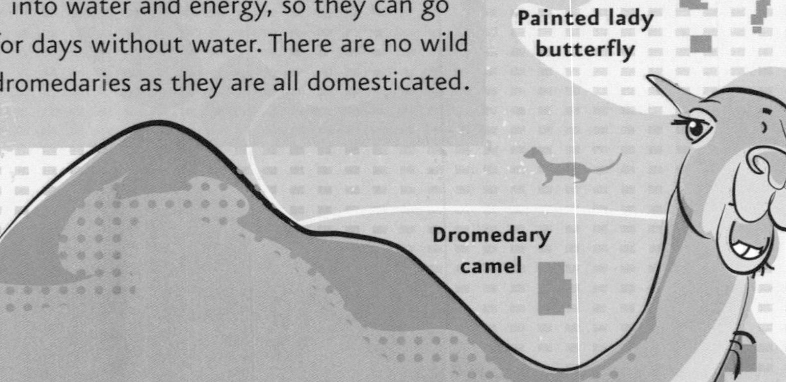

Cairo Zoo is home to a variety of resident and migrating birds, including colourful **little green** and **blue-cheeked bee-eaters**.

Blue-cheeked bee-eater

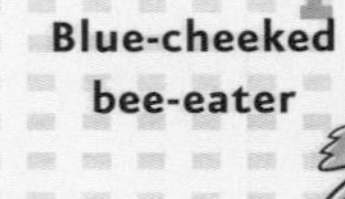

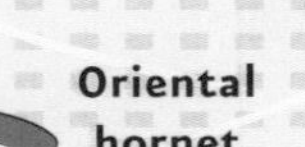

Oriental hornets have the unique ability to turn sunlight into energy!

Three types of **kingfisher** – the **pied**, the **white-breasted** and **common** – can be spotted in the city centre.

Crested lark

THE PYRAMIDS AND THE GREAT SPHINX OF GIZA

Jerboas have long back legs, allowing them to jump using their tails for balance. Nocturnal desert dwellers, they have been seen near the pyramids.

Common kestrel

Pallid swift

Fast-flying **pallid swifts** can be seen all over the city. They eat, sleep and mate while flying, only landing to nest.

Ancient Egyptians mummified **kestrels** and other falcons as offerings to the gods. Today, there is a pair of kestrels nesting at the American University in Cairo campus.

MEDITERRANEAN SEA

EGYPT

RED SEA

Lesser mouse-tailed bat

There are over 20 species of **bats** in Egypt. Some live in the heart of Cairo, roosting in old tunnels as well as in temples and mosques.

Lesser Egyptian gerbil

NASR CITY

AIRPORT
GREEN SPACES
ZOO
ANIMAL SIGHTINGS

AL AZHAR PARK

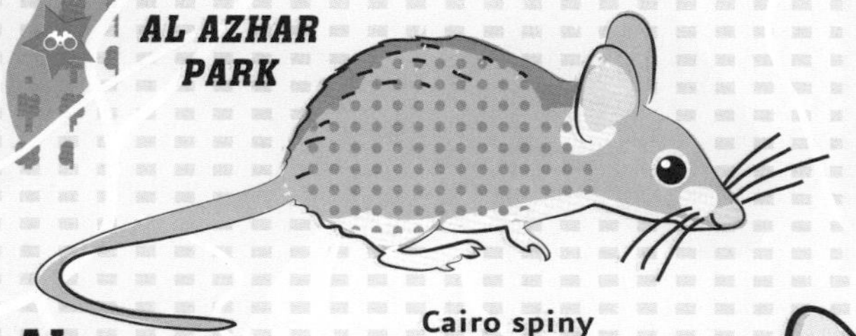

The **Cairo spiny mouse** can be found in people's homes. When scared, it raises spikes along its back to make it look bigger. It can even shed its tail like a lizard!

THE AMERICAN UNIVERSITY IN CAIRO

Egyptian weasel

AL ABAJIYYAH

Cairo spiny mouse

Stray cat

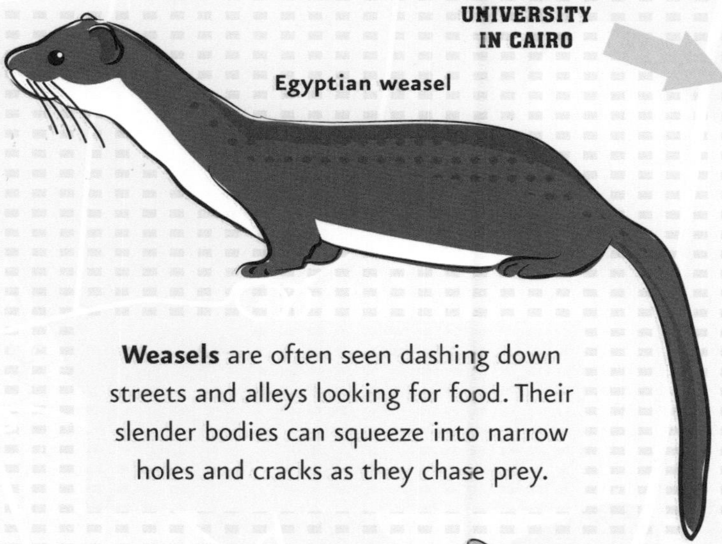

Weasels are often seen dashing down streets and alleys looking for food. Their slender bodies can squeeze into narrow holes and cracks as they chase prey.

ANIMAL STORIES

MAU MIAOW

Egypt has a unique breed of cat called the 'Egyptian Mau' which is likely to be one of the oldest breeds of domesticated cats, descended from its ancient Egyptian ancestors. Cats were beloved and worshipped as the goddess Bastet in ancient Egypt. Millions of mummified cats have been found in cat cemeteries throughout Egypt.

Today, Cairo is full of stray cats, many of which have the striking features of the Mau breed, with green eyes and striped and spotted fur.

Egyptian fan-footed gecko

Cape hares live throughout the open desert, including the Wadi Degla Nature Reserve near the city.

Cape hare

WADI DEGLA NATURE RESERVE

Can you find the 10 hidden weasels?

ADDIS ABABA

Ethiopia's capital sits high above sea level, at the foot of Mount Entoto. The ancient forest that covers the mountain slopes has been the training ground for some of Ethiopia's most famous long-distance runners. The city below is rich in birdlife, with lots of tropical species in parks, gardens and hotel grounds. At night, the eerie cackling of hyenas can be heard, and the odd leopard may even be seen in the shadows.

HYENA'S SPOTS

When the sun has set and everyone is asleep, groups of hyenas slink into the city to search for scraps of food, usually waste and bones left behind by people. By morning the hyenas have gone back to the outskirts and surrounding forests to sleep off their nightly feasts.

With a bite stronger than a great white shark's, these dangerous predators can chomp right through bone. But while hyenas are feared by many people across Africa, there is a long tradition of living side-by-side with them in Ethiopia. Attacks on people are very rare, and in some parts of the country people even feed the animals by hand!

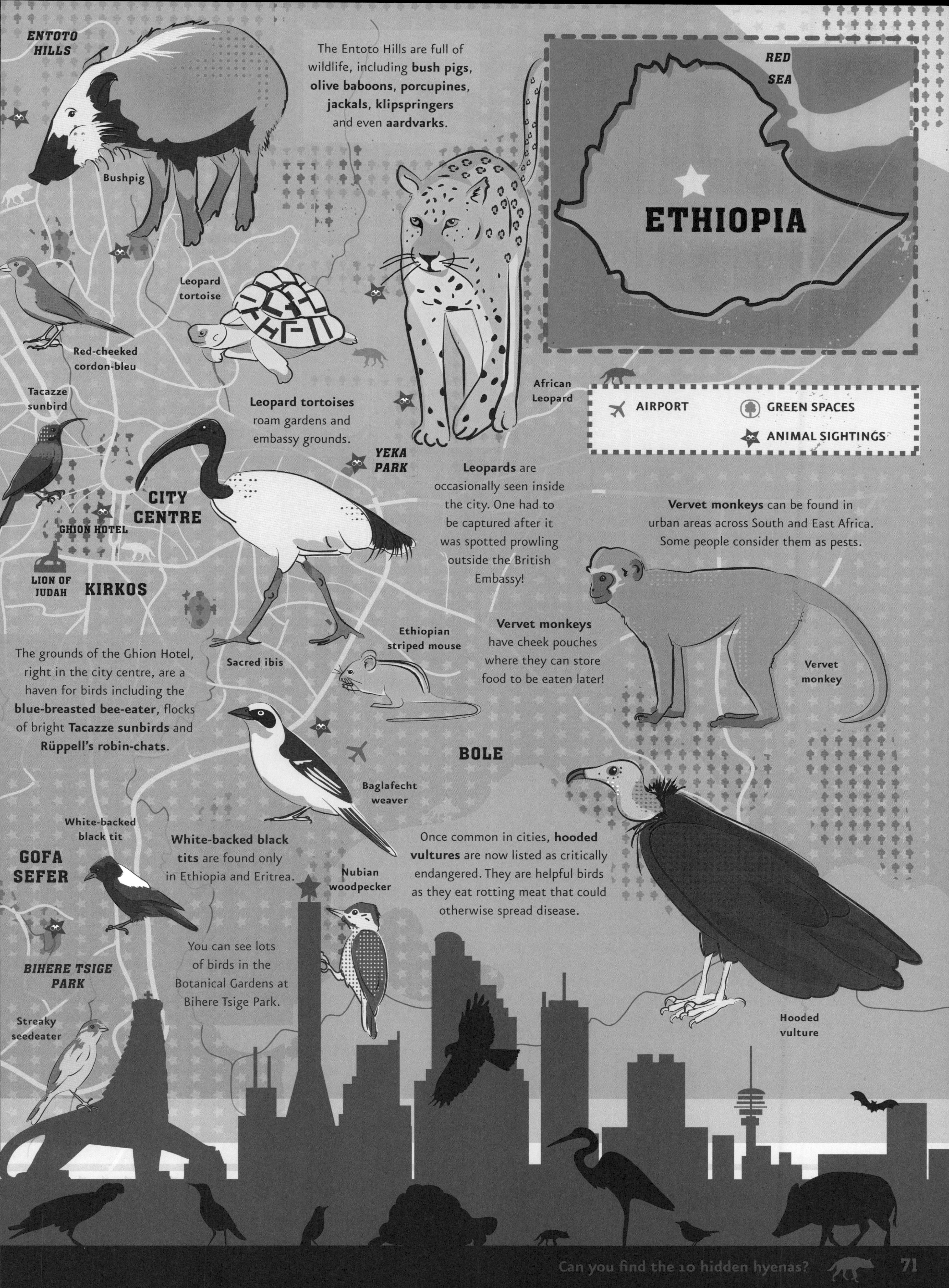
ENTOTO HILLS
The Entoto Hills are full of wildlife, including **bush pigs, olive baboons, porcupines, jackals, klipspringers** and even **aardvarks**.
RED SEA
ETHIOPIA
Bushpig
Leopard tortoise
Red-cheeked cordon-bleu
Tacazze sunbird
African Leopard
AIRPORT
GREEN SPACES
ANIMAL SIGHTINGS
Leopard tortoises roam gardens and embassy grounds.
YEKA PARK
CITY CENTRE
GHION HOTEL
LION OF JUDAH
KIRKOS
Leopards are occasionally seen inside the city. One had to be captured after it was spotted prowling outside the British Embassy!
Vervet monkeys can be found in urban areas across South and East Africa. Some people consider them as pests.
Ethiopian striped mouse
Vervet monkeys have cheek pouches where they can store food to be eaten later!
Vervet monkey
The grounds of the Ghion Hotel, right in the city centre, are a haven for birds including the **blue-breasted bee-eater**, flocks of bright **Tacazze sunbirds** and **Rüppell's robin-chats**.
Sacred ibis
BOLE
Baglafecht weaver
White-backed black tit
White-backed black tits are found only in Ethiopia and Eritrea.
GOFA SEFER
Nubian woodpecker
Once common in cities, **hooded vultures** are now listed as critically endangered. They are helpful birds as they eat rotting meat that could otherwise spread disease.
You can see lots of birds in the Botanical Gardens at Bihere Tsige Park.
BIHERE TSIGE PARK
Streaky seedeater
Hooded vulture
Can you find the 10 hidden hyenas?

NAIROBI

Nicknamed the safari capital of the world, Nairobi is the only metropolis to have a game reserve within its boundaries. Roaming giraffes, prides of lions and endangered black rhinos are all within viewing distance, while monkeys and baboons frequent the inner-city parks. You can see birds of prey circling overhead and on a clear day you can even see Africa's tallest mountain, Mount Kilimanjaro in neighbouring Tanzania.

African crowned eagle

Back from the brink of disappearing in the region, the **African crowned eagle** is a good indicator of a healthy forest and ecosystem.

LORESHO

Jackson's chameleon

Jackson's chameleon is found in wooded suburbs and back gardens. Like all chameleons, it can change its body colour!

Lion

Black kite

KAREN

NGONG FOREST SANCTUARY

Hadada ibis

KING OF THE BEASTS

Known as one of the 'big five' animals in Africa, lions are the top predators on the savannah grasslands. They are social animals which live in groups called prides, with the females working together to hunt. Like domestic cats they also like to laze around and sleep for up to 16 hours a day!

In recent years there have been increasing incidents of Nairobi National Park's lions wandering into urban areas. Past escapes have stopped traffic as lions end up on major roads. Sadly, when lions and humans come into contact, it is usually the lion that comes off worse. More education is needed to handle such encounters if both species are to survive living side-by-side.

ANIMAL STORIES

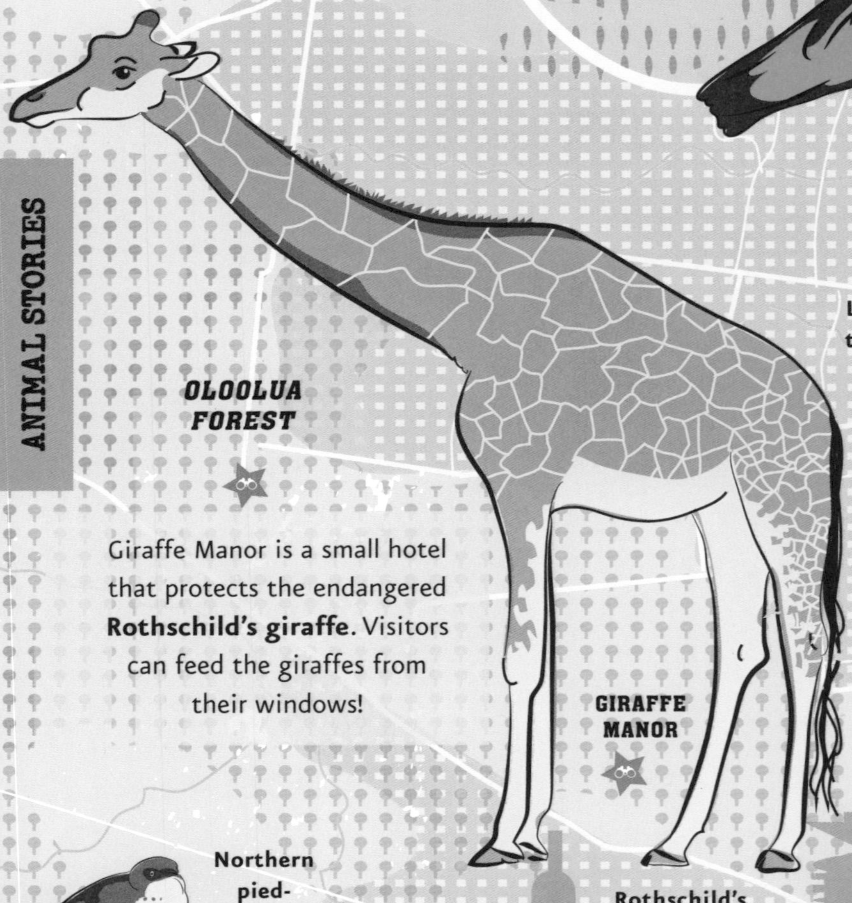

OLOOLUA FOREST

Giraffe Manor is a small hotel that protects the endangered **Rothschild's giraffe**. Visitors can feed the giraffes from their windows!

GIRAFFE MANOR

Rothschild's giraffe

Northern pied-babbler

NAIROBI ANIMAL ORPHANAGE

Leopard tortoise

The David Sheldrick Wildlife Trust has raise 150 orphan **elephant** from all over Africa.

DAVID SHELDRICK WILDLIFE TRUST

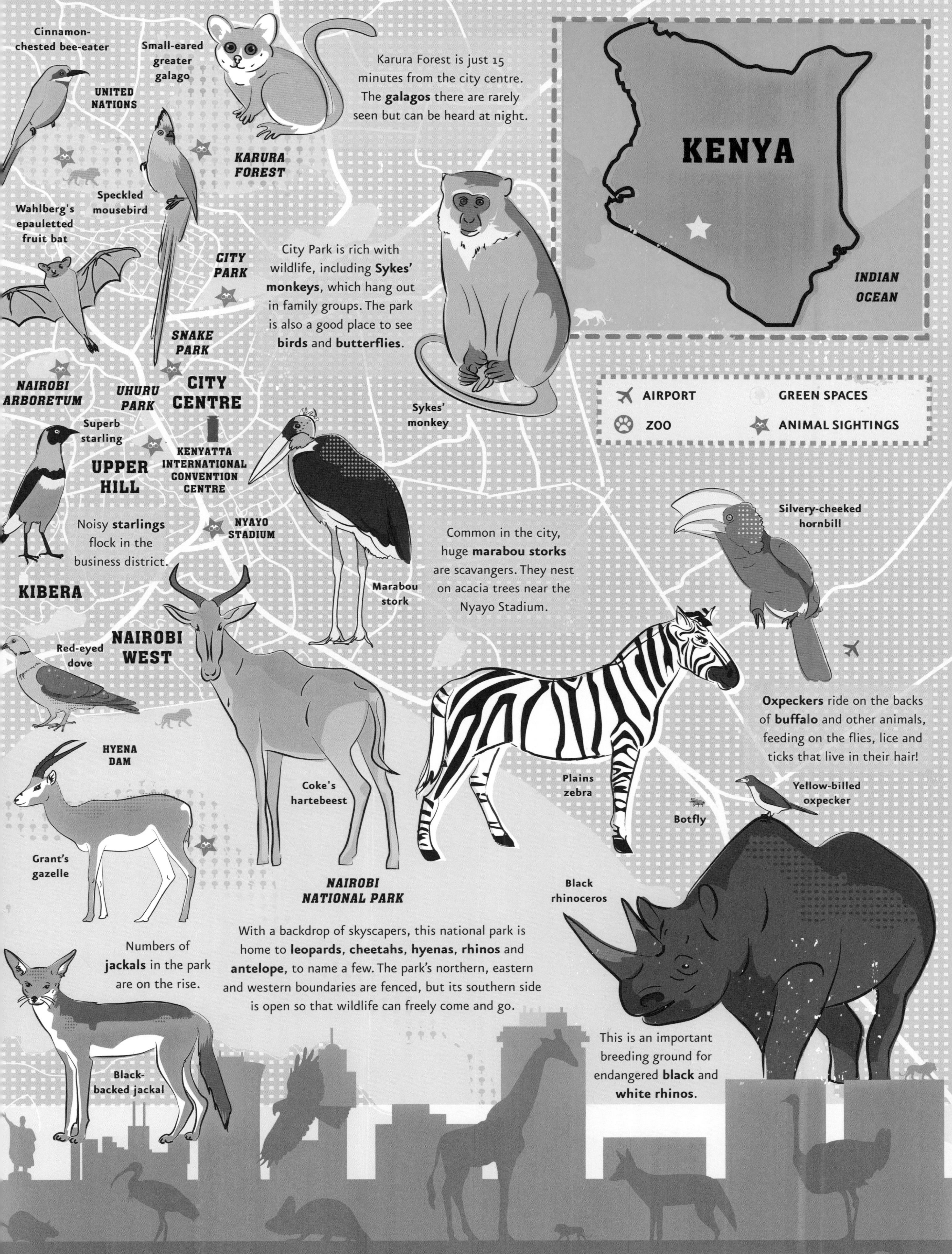

Cinnamon-chested bee-eater
Small-eared greater galago
UNITED NATIONS
Karura Forest is just 15 minutes from the city centre. The **galagos** there are rarely seen but can be heard at night.
KARURA FOREST
KENYA
INDIAN OCEAN
Speckled mousebird
Wahlberg's epauletted fruit bat
City Park is rich with wildlife, including **Sykes' monkeys**, which hang out in family groups. The park is also a good place to see **birds** and **butterflies**.
CITY PARK
SNAKE PARK
NAIROBI ARBORETUM
UHURU PARK
CITY CENTRE
Sykes' monkey
AIRPORT
GREEN SPACES
ZOO
ANIMAL SIGHTINGS
Superb starling
UPPER HILL
KENYATTA INTERNATIONAL CONVENTION CENTRE
NYAYO STADIUM
Noisy **starlings** flock in the business district.
KIBERA
Common in the city, huge **marabou storks** are scavangers. They nest on acacia trees near the Nyayo Stadium.
Marabou stork
Silvery-cheeked hornbill
Red-eyed dove
NAIROBI WEST
Oxpeckers ride on the backs of **buffalo** and other animals, feeding on the flies, lice and ticks that live in their hair!
HYENA DAM
Coke's hartebeest
Plains zebra
Botfly
Yellow-billed oxpecker
Grant's gazelle
NAIROBI NATIONAL PARK
Black rhinoceros
Numbers of **jackals** in the park are on the rise.
With a backdrop of skyscapers, this national park is home to **leopards**, **cheetahs**, **hyenas**, **rhinos** and **antelope**, to name a few. The park's northern, eastern and western boundaries are fenced, but its southern side is open so that wildlife can freely come and go.
This is an important breeding ground for endangered **black** and **white rhinos**.
Black-backed jackal
Can you find the 10 hidden lions?

GABORONE

Gaborone is a young city, built as a new capital in the 1960s after Botswana gained its independence from Great Britain. Affectionately known as 'Gabs', it is generally regarded as a safe, prosperous place, and is still rapidly growing. The large dam above the city was built to provide the area with water, but is also a popular fishing spot and home to plenty of wildlife. Just watch out for the occasional crocodile!

African darter

EXTENSION 36

BLOCK 7

The **African darter** is also called the 'snakebird' because of the way it swims with just its long neck and head showing above the water.

Vervet monkey

THREE DIKGOSI MONUMENT

BUSINESS DISTRICT

Rock hyrax

Rock hyraxes, also known as 'rock dassies', love to sunbathe together.

SEGODITSHANE RIVER

ROCK-HOPPING HYRAXES

The rock hyrax may look like a cross between a guinea pig and a rabbit, but in fact it is most closely related to the elephant. The little animal even has tiny tusk-like upper teeth!

Hyraxes are certainly not your average animal... Their padded, sweaty feet act like suction cups, helping them to cling to the rock faces they live on. They also have three stomachs! Hyraxes communicate using bizarre sounds like snorts, shrieks, whistles and grunts. Big groups live on Kgale Hill and around the Gaborone Dam area.

ANIMAL STORIES

A troop of **baboons** lives on Kgale Hill, one of the city's biggest landmarks. There have even been early-morning sightings of **leopards** on the hill.

Cheeky **vervet monkeys** live in the green areas of the city, including hotel gardens, the Game Reserve and the Botanical Garden.

African monarch butterfly

African paradise flycatcher

Gaborone Dam is an important feature in this drought-prone region. The reservoir is a haven for water birds like **purple herons, great white egrets** and **giant kingfishers**.

African leopard

Chacma baboon

GAME CITY

OLD NALEDI

Black eagle

KGALE HILL

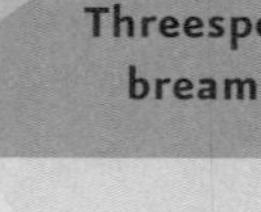

Impressive **black eagles** nest on Kgale Hill.

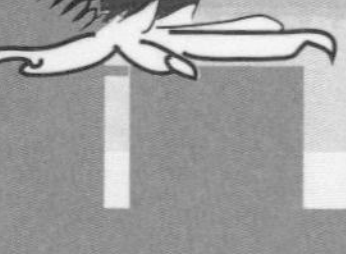

Threespot bream

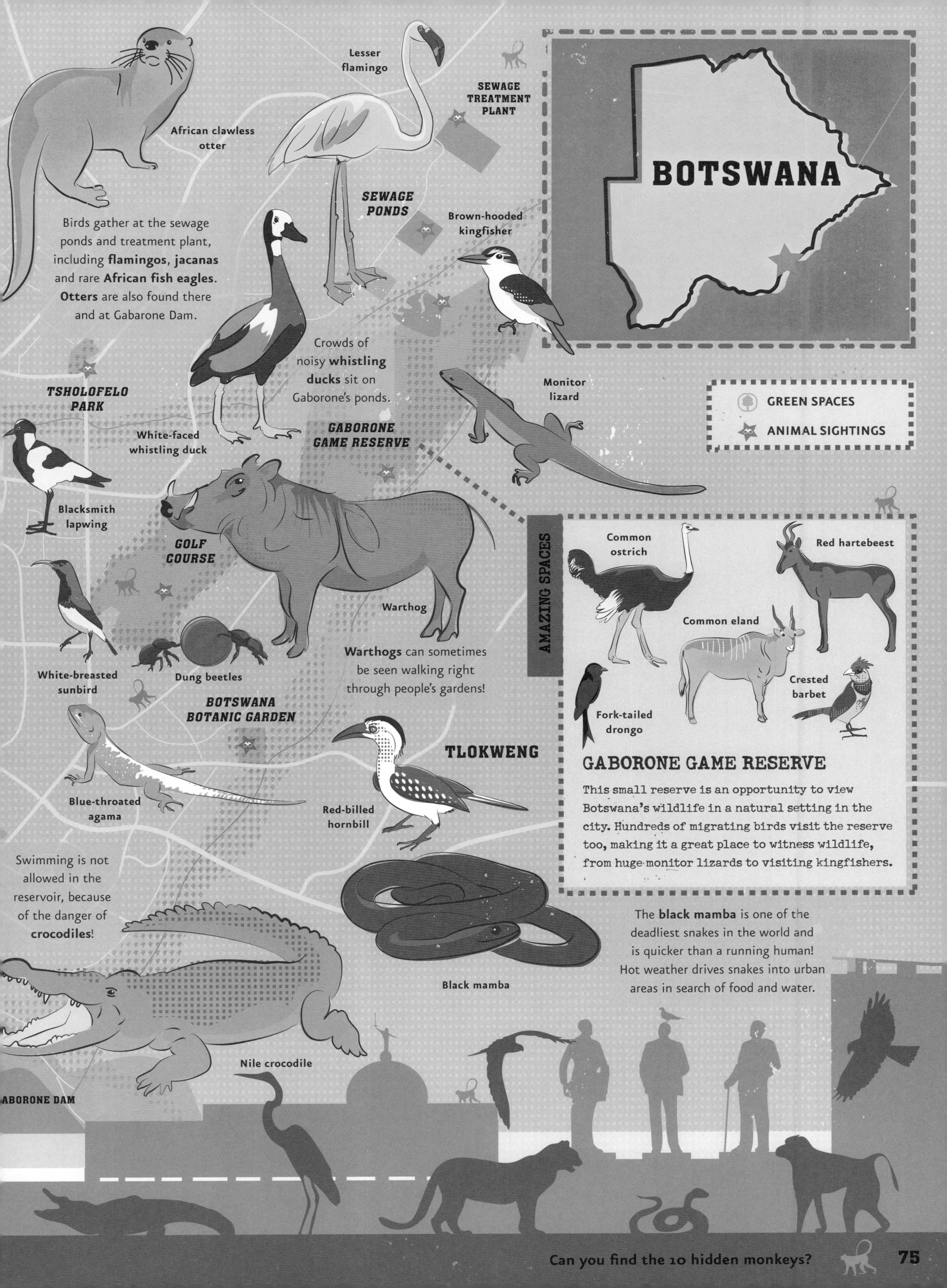
Lesser flamingo
African clawless otter
SEWAGE TREATMENT PLANT
BOTSWANA
SEWAGE PONDS
Brown-hooded kingfisher
Birds gather at the sewage ponds and treatment plant, including **flamingos, jacanas** and rare **African fish eagles. Otters** are also found there and at Gabarone Dam.
Crowds of noisy **whistling ducks** sit on Gaborone's ponds.
Monitor lizard
TSHOLOFELO PARK
GREEN SPACES
ANIMAL SIGHTINGS
White-faced whistling duck
GABORONE GAME RESERVE
Blacksmith lapwing
GOLF COURSE
AMAZING SPACES
Common ostrich
Red hartebeest
Warthog
Common eland
White-breasted sunbird
Dung beetles
Warthogs can sometimes be seen walking right through people's gardens!
Crested barbet
Fork-tailed drongo
BOTSWANA BOTANIC GARDEN
TLOKWENG
GABORONE GAME RESERVE
This small reserve is an opportunity to view Botswana's wildlife in a natural setting in the city. Hundreds of migrating birds visit the reserve too, making it a great place to witness wildlife, from huge monitor lizards to visiting kingfishers.
Blue-throated agama
Red-billed hornbill
Swimming is not allowed in the reservoir, because of the danger of **crocodiles**!
The **black mamba** is one of the deadliest snakes in the world and is quicker than a running human! Hot weather drives snakes into urban areas in search of food and water.
Black mamba
Nile crocodile
ABORONE DAM
Can you find the 10 hidden monkeys?

CAPE TOWN

The bustling city of Cape Town sweeps down from the flat top of Table Mountain to the Atlantic Ocean below. The plant life in this area – scrubland known as 'fynbos' – is one of the richest ecosystems in the world. The rooibos or 'red bush' plant, whose leaves are made into tea, is found here. The city offers some incredible wildlife experiences both on land and at sea: visitors can dive with sharks, meet monkeys or encounter playful penguins.

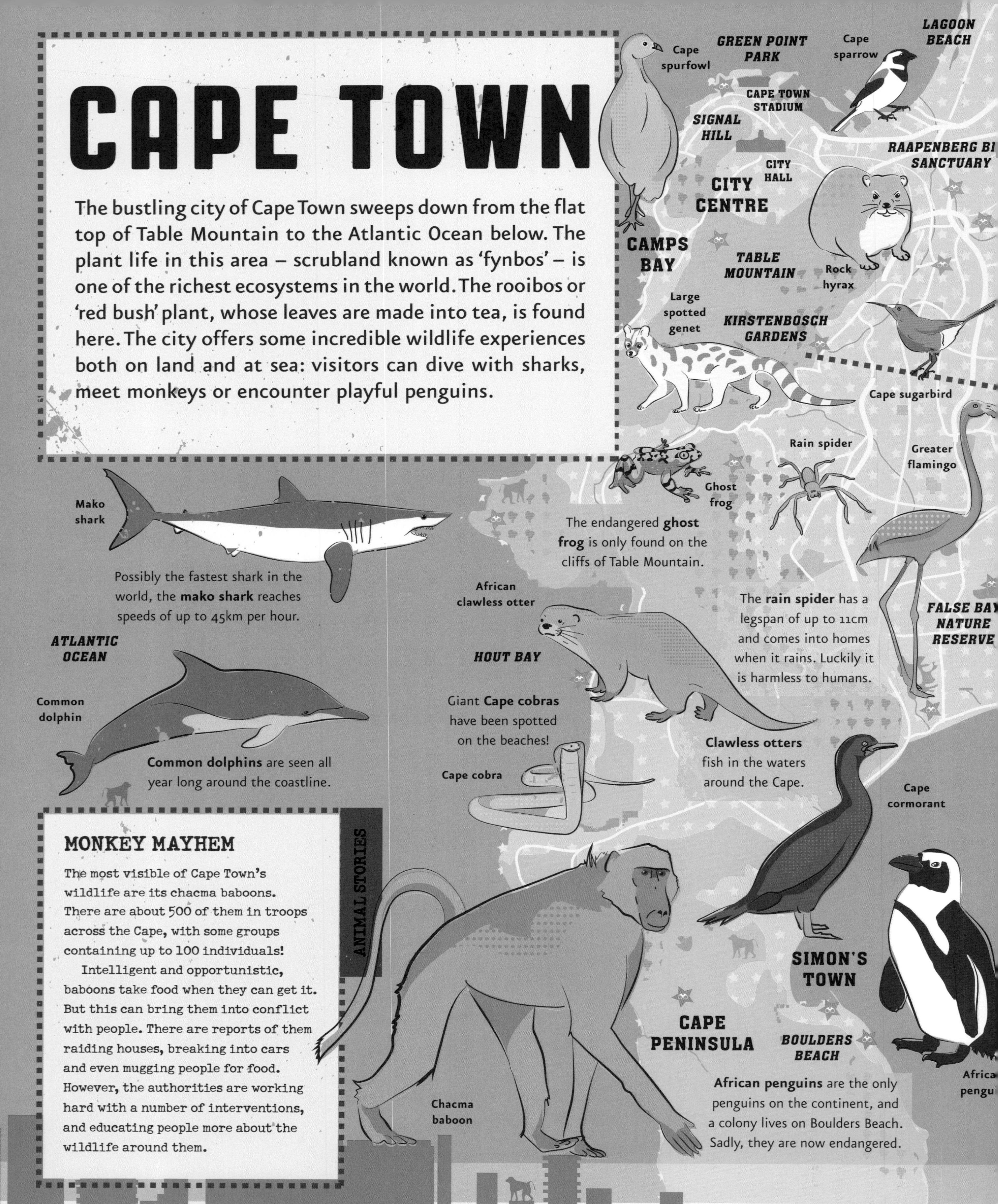

The endangered **ghost frog** is only found on the cliffs of Table Mountain.

Possibly the fastest shark in the world, the **mako shark** reaches speeds of up to 45km per hour.

The **rain spider** has a legspan of up to 11cm and comes into homes when it rains. Luckily it is harmless to humans.

Giant **Cape cobras** have been spotted on the beaches!

Clawless otters fish in the waters around the Cape.

Common dolphins are seen all year long around the coastline.

African penguins are the only penguins on the continent, and a colony lives on Boulders Beach. Sadly, they are now endangered.

ANIMAL STORIES

MONKEY MAYHEM

The most visible of Cape Town's wildlife are its chacma baboons. There are about 500 of them in troops across the Cape, with some groups containing up to 100 individuals!

Intelligent and opportunistic, baboons take food when they can get it. But this can bring them into conflict with people. There are reports of them raiding houses, breaking into cars and even mugging people for food. However, the authorities are working hard with a number of interventions, and educating people more about the wildlife around them.

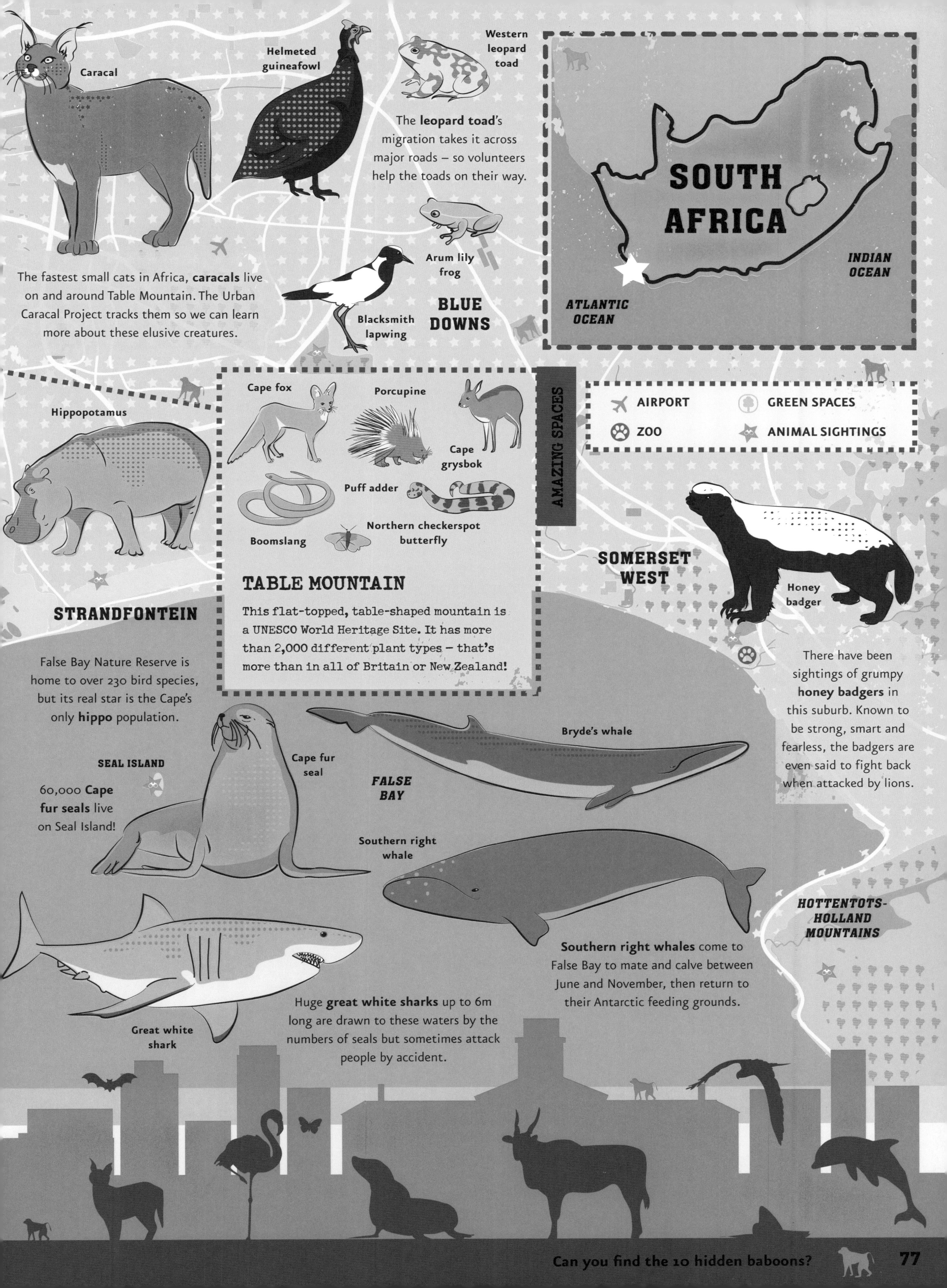
Caracal
Helmeted guineafowl
Western leopard toad
The leopard toad's migration takes it across major roads – so volunteers help the toads on their way.
SOUTH AFRICA
INDIAN OCEAN
ATLANTIC OCEAN
Arum lily frog
Blacksmith lapwing
BLUE DOWNS
The fastest small cats in Africa, caracals live on and around Table Mountain. The Urban Caracal Project tracks them so we can learn more about these elusive creatures.
AMAZING SPACES
Cape fox
Porcupine
Cape grysbok
Puff adder
Boomslang
Northern checkerspot butterfly
TABLE MOUNTAIN
This flat-topped, table-shaped mountain is a UNESCO World Heritage Site. It has more than 2,000 different plant types – that's more than in all of Britain or New Zealand!
AIRPORT
GREEN SPACES
ZOO
ANIMAL SIGHTINGS
Hippopotamus
STRANDFONTEIN
False Bay Nature Reserve is home to over 230 bird species, but its real star is the Cape's only hippo population.
SOMERSET WEST
Honey badger
There have been sightings of grumpy honey badgers in this suburb. Known to be strong, smart and fearless, the badgers are even said to fight back when attacked by lions.
SEAL ISLAND
60,000 Cape fur seals live on Seal Island!
Cape fur seal
FALSE BAY
Bryde's whale
Southern right whale
HOTTENTOTS-HOLLAND MOUNTAINS
Southern right whales come to False Bay to mate and calve between June and November, then return to their Antarctic feeding grounds.
Huge great white sharks up to 6m long are drawn to these waters by the numbers of seals but sometimes attack people by accident.
Great white shark
Can you find the 10 hidden baboons?
77

ASIA

Asia is the biggest continent in the world and is home to more variety of plant and animal species than any other continent. Crowded cities and pollution are just some of the challenges facing nature here, but an incredible array of animals still crowd alongside people into urban settings. In some places, animals are revered and their presence is even seen as a blessing.

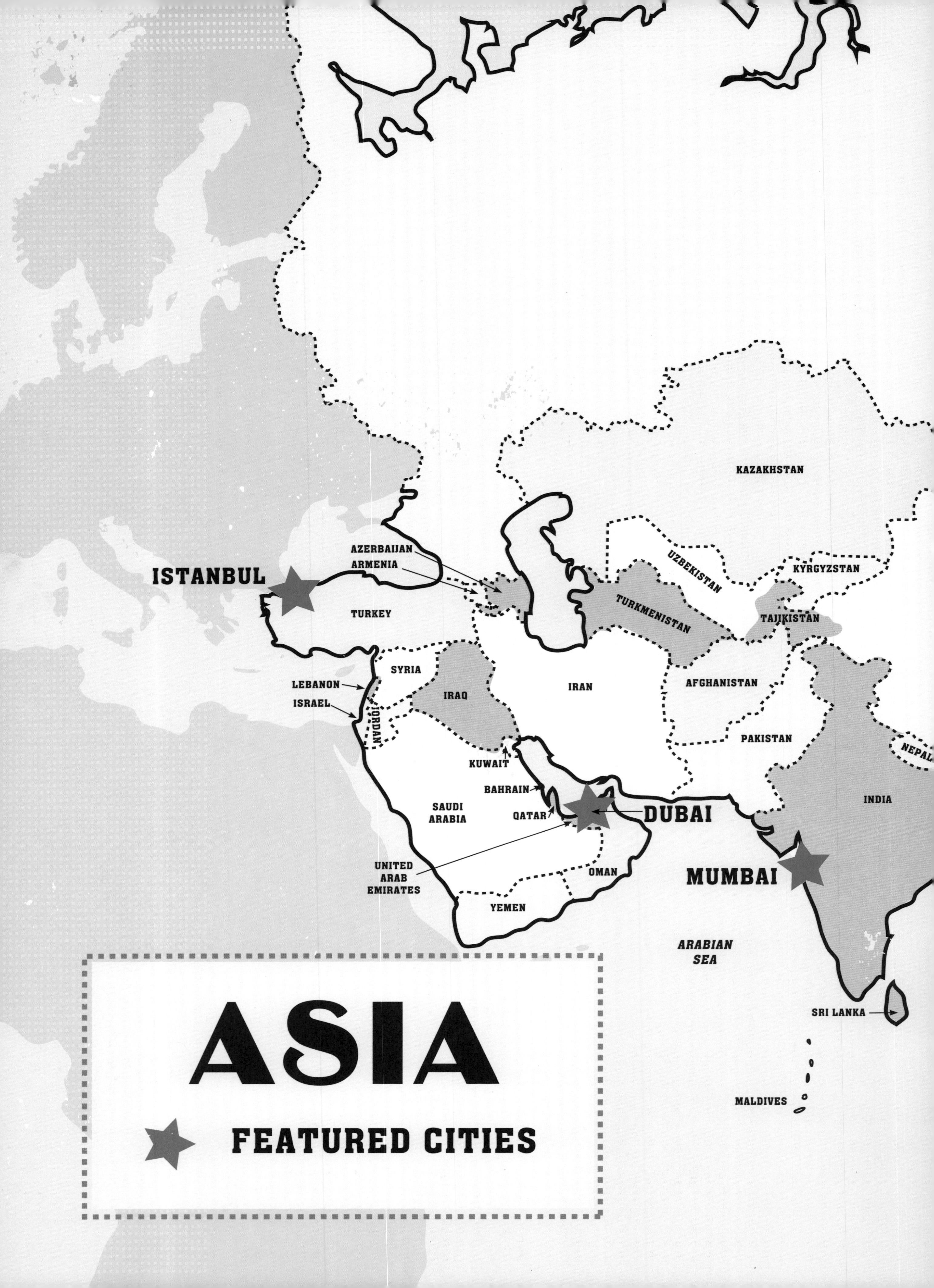
ASIA
FEATURED CITIES
ISTANBUL
DUBAI
MUMBAI
KAZAKHSTAN
UZBEKISTAN
KYRGYZSTAN
TURKMENISTAN
TAJIKISTAN
AZERBAIJAN
ARMENIA
TURKEY
SYRIA
LEBANON
ISRAEL
JORDAN
IRAQ
IRAN
AFGHANISTAN
PAKISTAN
NEPAL
INDIA
KUWAIT
BAHRAIN
QATAR
SAUDI ARABIA
UNITED ARAB EMIRATES
OMAN
YEMEN
ARABIAN SEA
SRI LANKA
MALDIVES

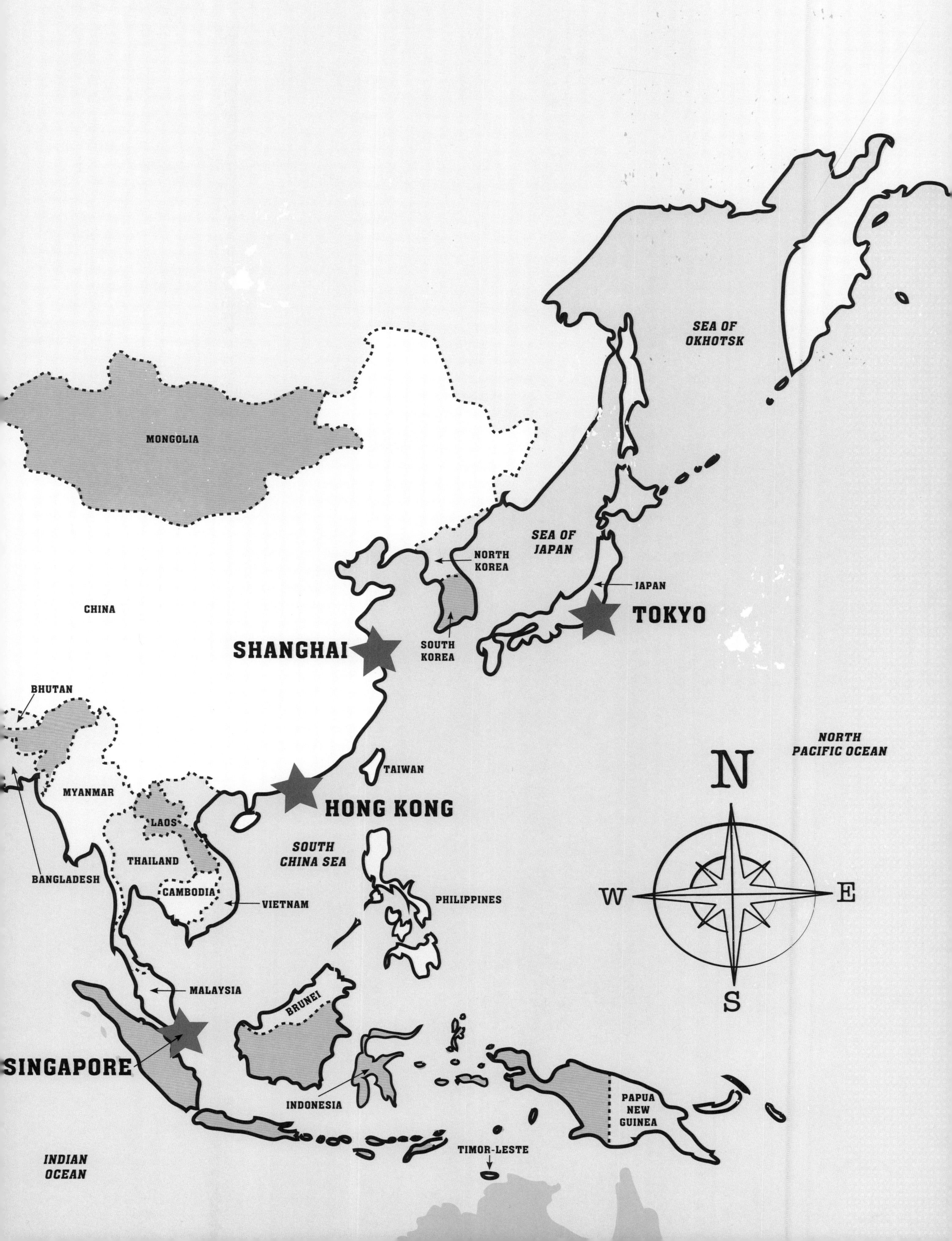
SEA OF OKHOTSK
MONGOLIA
SEA OF JAPAN
NORTH KOREA
JAPAN
CHINA
TOKYO
SHANGHAI
SOUTH KOREA
BHUTAN
NORTH PACIFIC OCEAN
N
TAIWAN
MYANMAR
HONG KONG
LAOS
SOUTH CHINA SEA
THAILAND
BANGLADESH
CAMBODIA
VIETNAM
W
E
PHILIPPINES
MALAYSIA
S
BRUNEI
SINGAPORE
INDONESIA
PAPUA NEW GUINEA
TIMOR-LESTE
INDIAN OCEAN

ISTANBUL

This ancient city straddles the Bosphorus Strait, a stretch of water dividing the continents of Europe and Asia. Its centre shows traces of the empires that once ruled here, with Roman ruins alongside Ottoman mosques and Byzantine churches. This point where east meets west is on the migration route for many birds. The city's waters, though busy with traffic, are still home to seahorses, dolphins and thousands of jellyfish!

Common buzzard

Ring-necked parakeet

Caucasian squirrels live in the trees of Yıldız Park.

Beech martens look for berries and birds' eggs in the gardens of the Hilton Hotel near Taksim Square.

Wild boar

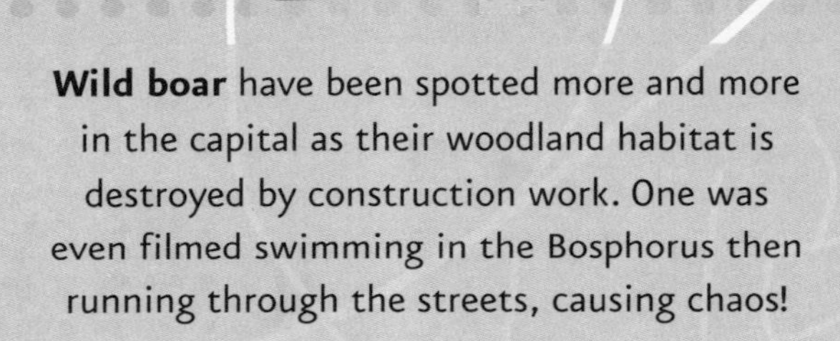

Wild boar have been spotted more and more in the capital as their woodland habitat is destroyed by construction work. One was even filmed swimming in the Bosphorus then running through the streets, causing chaos!

Once full of marine life, the Bosphorus Strait is now a busy shipping corridor. Despite the efforts of wildlife charities, pollution, overfishing and boat collision are threatening the area's **dolphins** and **porpoises**.

Bottlenose dolphin

Yelkouan shearwater

Harbour porpoise

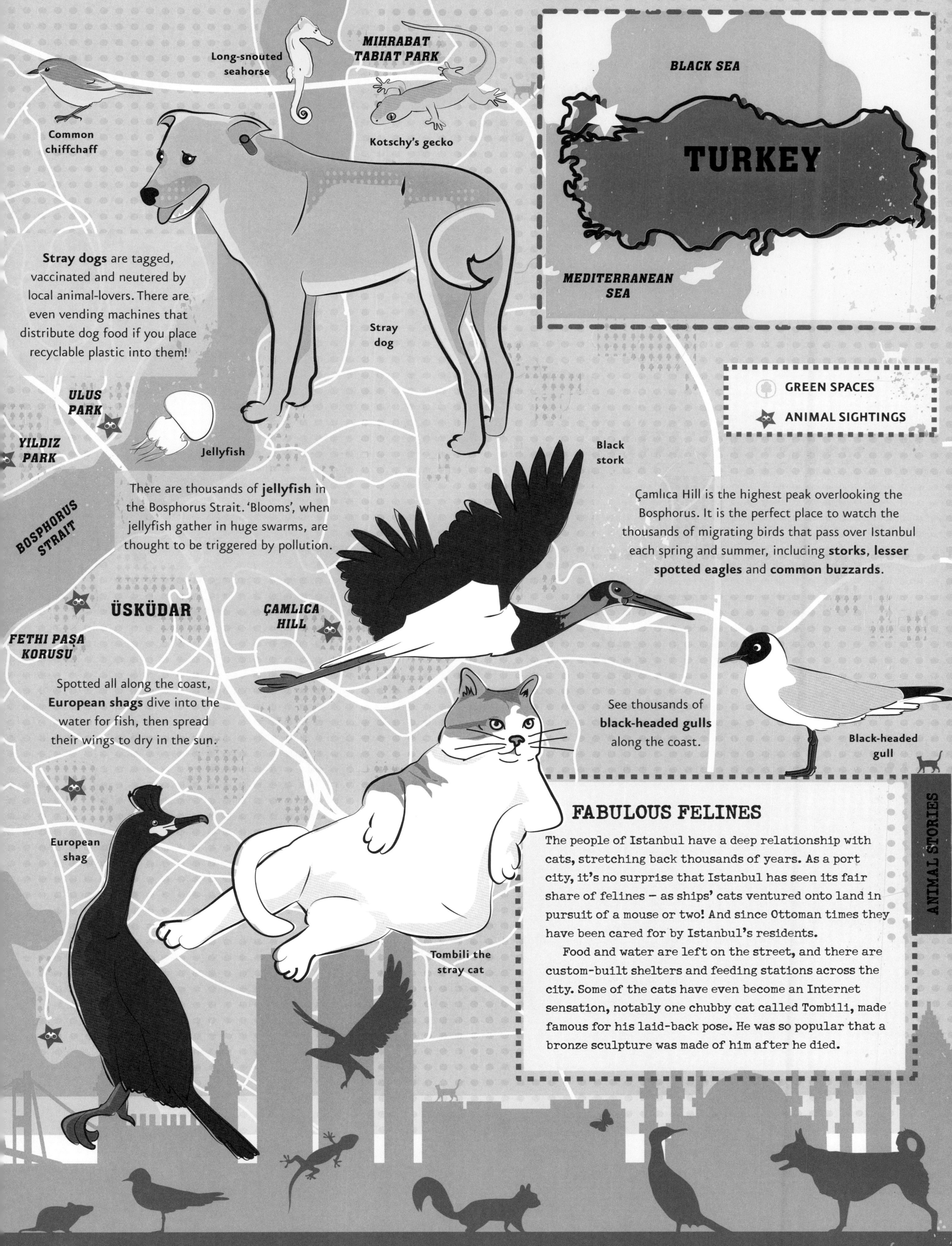

Stray dogs are tagged, vaccinated and neutered by local animal-lovers. There are even vending machines that distribute dog food if you place recyclable plastic into them!

There are thousands of **jellyfish** in the Bosphorus Strait. 'Blooms', when jellyfish gather in huge swarms, are thought to be triggered by pollution.

Çamlıca Hill is the highest peak overlooking the Bosphorus. It is the perfect place to watch the thousands of migrating birds that pass over Istanbul each spring and summer, inclucing **storks, lesser spotted eagles** and **common buzzards**.

Spotted all along the coast, **European shags** dive into the water for fish, then spread their wings to dry in the sun.

See thousands of **black-headed gulls** along the coast.

FABULOUS FELINES

The people of Istanbul have a deep relationship with cats, stretching back thousands of years. As a port city, it's no surprise that Istanbul has seen its fair share of felines – as ships' cats ventured onto land in pursuit of a mouse or two! And since Ottoman times they have been cared for by Istanbul's residents.

Food and water are left on the street, and there are custom-built shelters and feeding stations across the city. Some of the cats have even become an Internet sensation, notably one chubby cat called Tombili, made famous for his laid-back pose. He was so popular that a bronze sculpture was made of him after he died.

Can you find the 10 hidden cats?

DUBAI

Dubai is the largest city in the United Arab Emirates (UAE), perhaps best known for its incredible construction projects: the 828m Burj Khalifa is the tallest building in the world, and the coastline has several man-made islands, including some shaped like palm trees! With increasing awareness of wildlife, projects are caring for the area's marine life, while on land there are some amazing places to spot migrating birds.

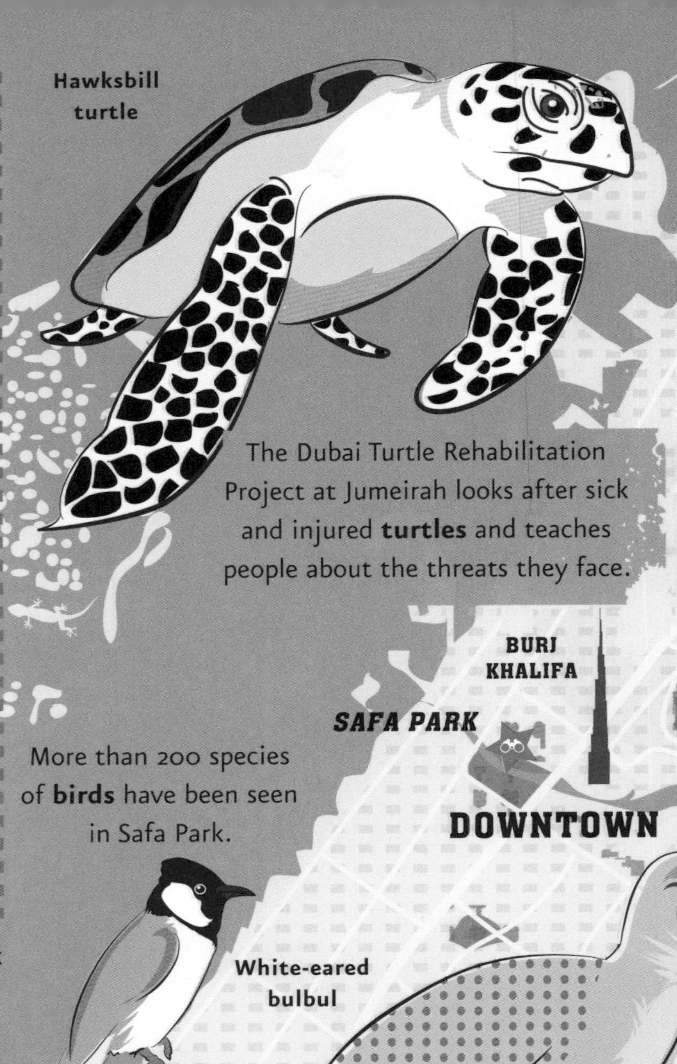

The Dubai Turtle Rehabilitation Project at Jumeirah looks after sick and injured **turtles** and teaches people about the threats they face.

More than 200 species of **birds** have been seen in Safa Park.

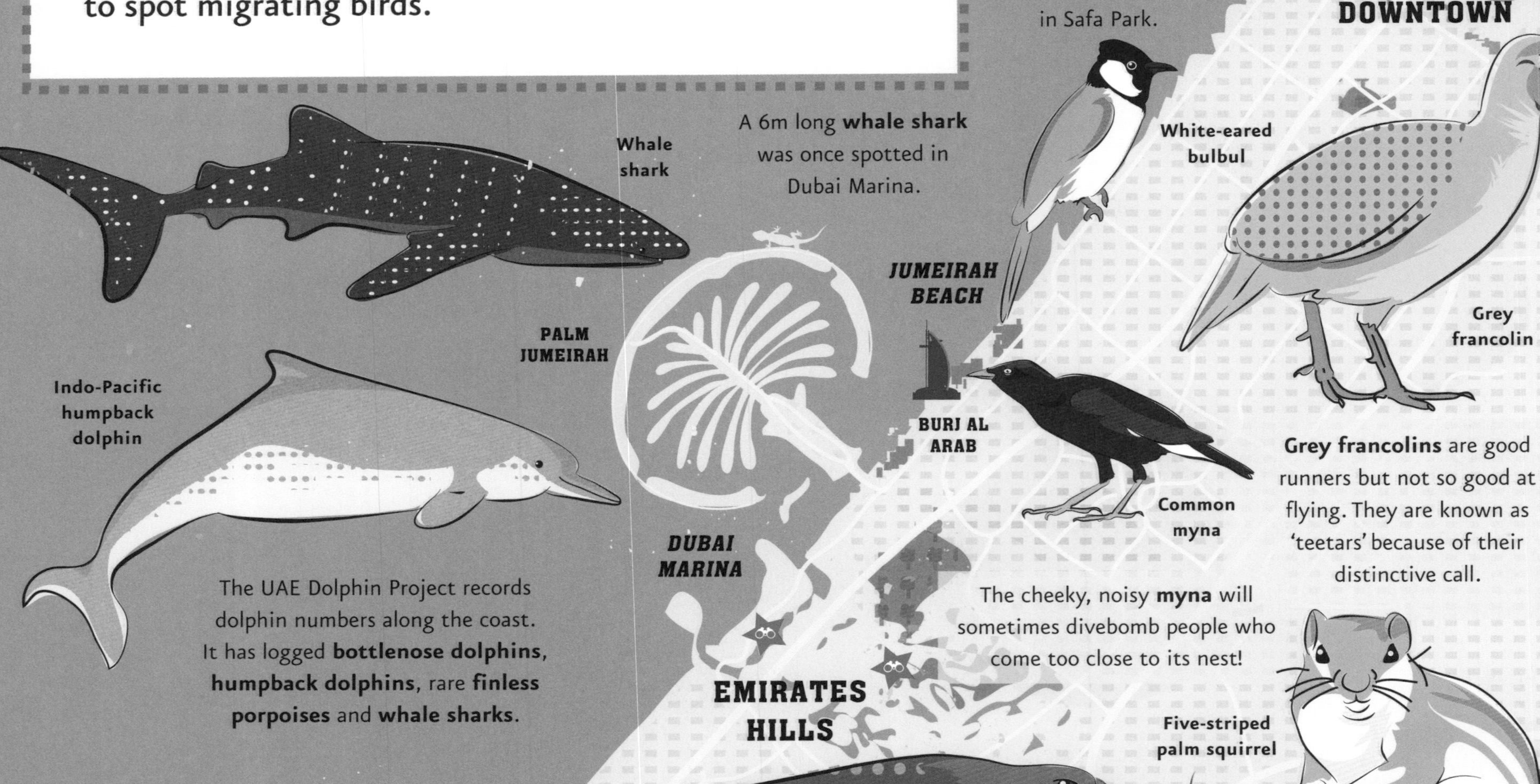

A 6m long **whale shark** was once spotted in Dubai Marina.

Grey francolins are good runners but not so good at flying. They are known as 'teetars' because of their distinctive call.

The UAE Dolphin Project records dolphin numbers along the coast. It has logged **bottlenose dolphins**, **humpback dolphins**, rare **finless porpoises** and **whale sharks**.

The cheeky, noisy **myna** will sometimes divebomb people who come too close to its nest!

The **western pygmy blue butterfly** is a native of North America but it thrives on garden plants across Dubai.

The cute **five-striped palm squirrel** is a native of India, but is found in Dubai's city parks.

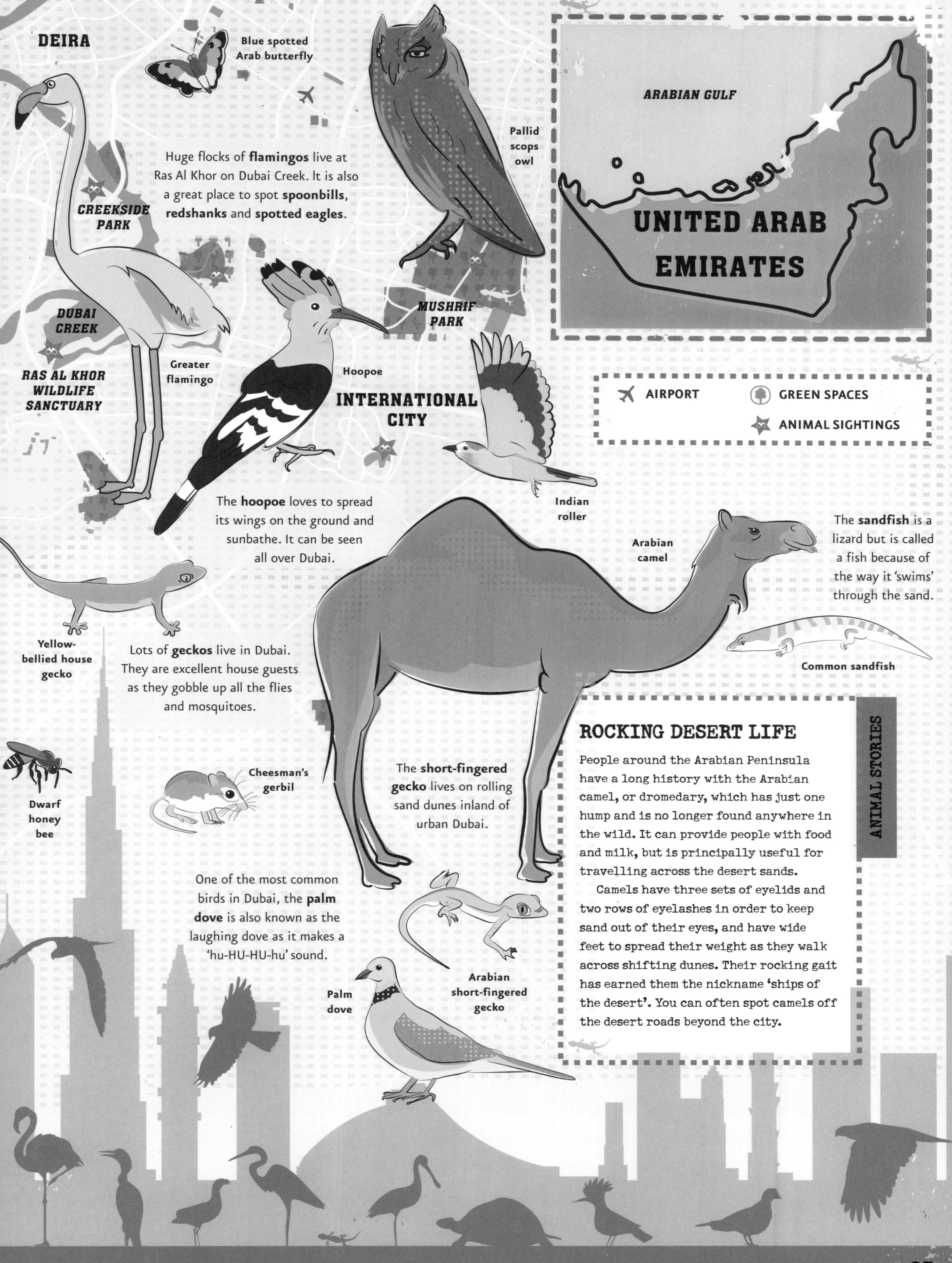

Huge flocks of **flamingos** live at Ras Al Khor on Dubai Creek. It is also a great place to spot **spoonbills**, **redshanks** and **spotted eagles**.

The **hoopoe** loves to spread its wings on the ground and sunbathe. It can be seen all over Dubai.

The **sandfish** is a lizard but is called a fish because of the way it 'swims' through the sand.

Lots of **geckos** live in Dubai. They are excellent house guests as they gobble up all the flies and mosquitoes.

The **short-fingered gecko** lives on rolling sand dunes inland of urban Dubai.

One of the most common birds in Dubai, the **palm dove** is also known as the laughing dove as it makes a 'hu-HU-HU-hu' sound.

ROCKING DESERT LIFE

People around the Arabian Peninsula have a long history with the Arabian camel, or dromedary, which has just one hump and is no longer found anywhere in the wild. It can provide people with food and milk, but is principally useful for travelling across the desert sands.

Camels have three sets of eyelids and two rows of eyelashes in order to keep sand out of their eyes, and have wide feet to spread their weight as they walk across shifting dunes. Their rocking gait has earned them the nickname **'ships of the desert'**. You can often spot camels off the desert roads beyond the city.

Can you find the 10 hidden geckos?

MUMBAI

On the west coast of India, Mumbai is the country's largest city and its financial capital. Its streets are a mix of sprawling slums and luxurious mansions, where all manner of wildlife roams. Wild cats wander the suburbs, crocodiles lurk in the lakes, and dangerous snakes can make their way into homes. The nearby ocean is just as busy – here you'll find turtles, sharks, dolphins and even migrating humpback whales.

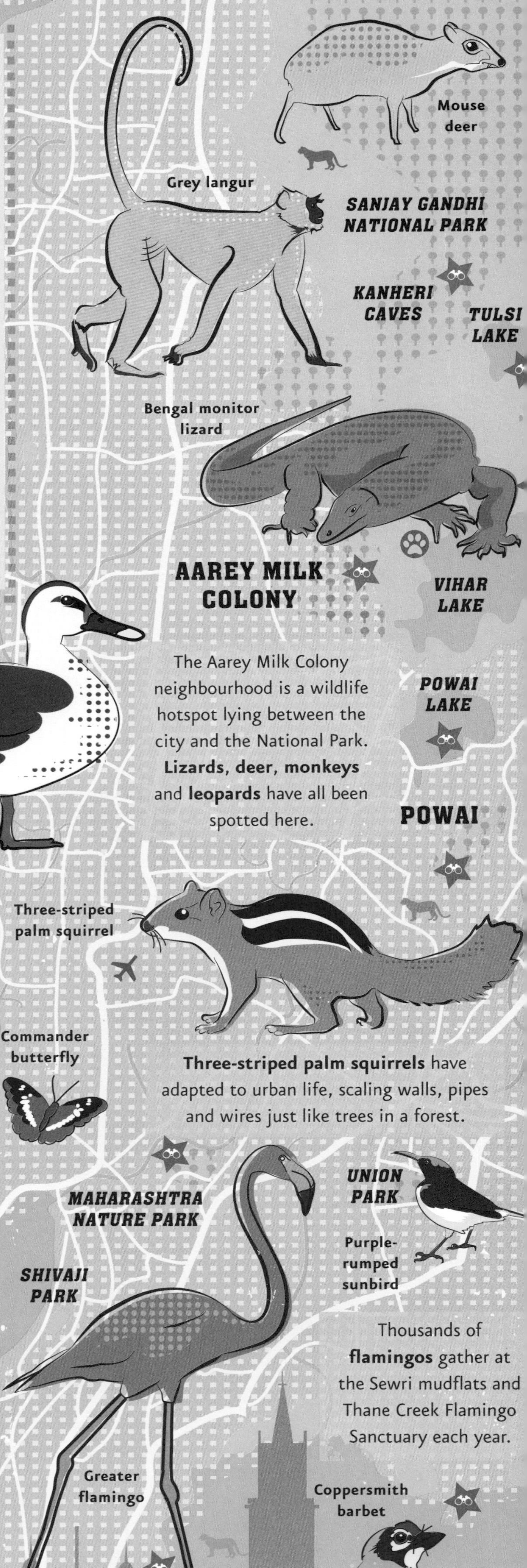

The Aarey Milk Colony neighbourhood is a wildlife hotspot lying between the city and the National Park. **Lizards, deer, monkeys** and **leopards** have all been spotted here.

Three-striped palm squirrels have adapted to urban life, scaling walls, pipes and wires just like trees in a forest.

Thousands of **flamingos** gather at the Sewri mudflats and Thane Creek Flamingo Sanctuary each year.

SILVER BEACH

LOKHANDWALA LAKE

Milk shark

Indian spot-billed duck

Humpback whales pass Mumbai on their migration to Antarctica.

Humpback whale

ARABIAN SEA

Maharashtra Nature Park is a 40-acre reserve that was once a city dump! It is home to around 120 species of birds, 75 species of butterflies, and various snakes, including **cobras**.

Green turtle

Indian cobra

The rare **humpback dolphin** can be spotted playing off the coast.

Indo-Pacific humpback dolphin

SOUTH MUMBAI

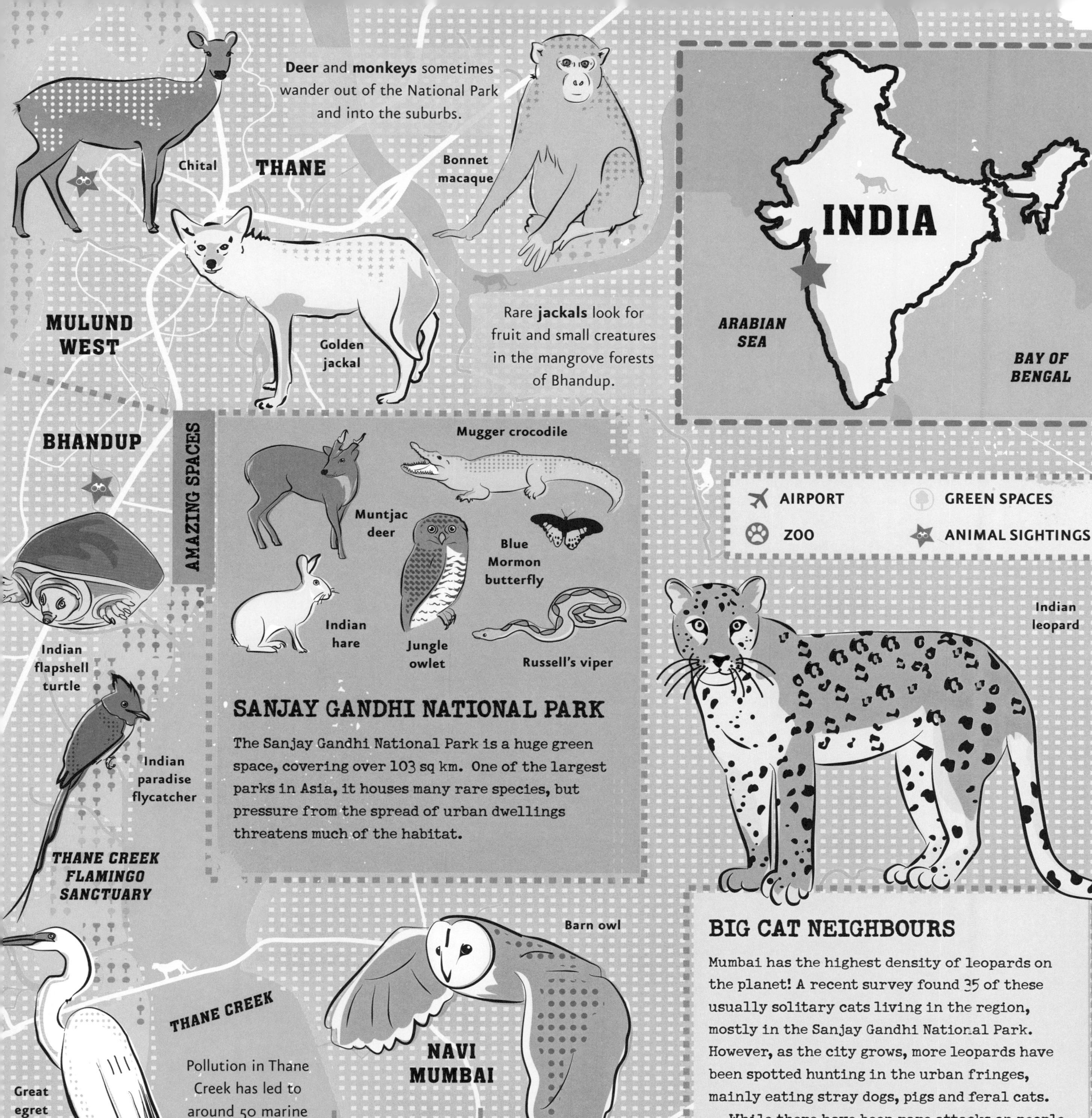

SANJAY GANDHI NATIONAL PARK

The Sanjay Gandhi National Park is a huge green space, covering over 103 sq km. One of the largest parks in Asia, it houses many rare species, but pressure from the spread of urban dwellings threatens much of the habitat.

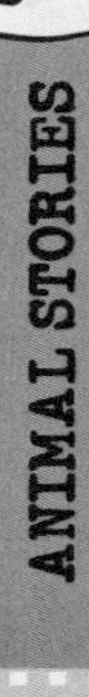

BIG CAT NEIGHBOURS

Mumbai has the highest density of leopards on the planet! A recent survey found 35 of these usually solitary cats living in the region, mostly in the Sanjay Gandhi National Park. However, as the city grows, more leopards have been spotted hunting in the urban fringes, mainly eating stray dogs, pigs and feral cats.

While there have been rare attacks on people, increasing public awareness, camera technology and forest keeper patrols have all helped to improve safety. Let's hope humans can adapt to this new arrangement like the leopards seem to have done.

Sharphead flyingfish

See large fruit bats known as **Indian flying foxes** roosting in the suburbs.

Indian flying fox

Can you find the 10 hidden leopards?

HONG KONG

Hong Kong is an international centre for business and finance, but beyond its towering skyscrapers, this sub-tropical metropolis has a green side. Over 40 per cent of Hong Kong's hilly land is covered in forests, grass and country parks, and its sprawling coastline offers several marine parks. Although species struggle for survival, a conservation plan hopes to preserve Hong Kong's wild neighbours as the city continues to grow.

TAI WAI

Leopard cat

LION ROCK COUNTRY PARK

Threatened **leopard cats** are found all over the Hong Kong region. They are rarely seen as they hunt at night.

Redbase Jezebel butterfly

Spotted dove

Japanese pipistrelle

The most common of Hong Kong's 27 bat species is the **Japanese pipistrelle**, which lives among high-rise buildings, and will even roost in air-conditioning units!

TSIM SHA TSUI

KOWLOON PARK

Pallas's squirrel

Indo-Pacific humpback dolphin

VICTORIA HARBOUR

TWO INTERNATIONAL FINANCE CENTRE

CENTRAL HONG KONG

CONVENTION CENTER

MID-LEVEL

IN THE PINK

ANIMAL STORIES

The Indo-Pacific humpback dolphin, also known as the Chinese white dolphin, has been living in the waters around Hong Kong for centuries. However, awareness of the dolphins has only started to grow since the 1990s, since when visitors have been able to watch their acrobatics from boat trips.

These incredible creatures are grey when they are born, then turn white or pink by adulthood. Sadly, the dolphins are struggling against overfishing, habitat loss and pollution. They also only breed every 4–6 years, which means their numbers are dwindling fast. A conservation programme is doing everything possible to protect these majestic animals and their habitat.

Light-vented bulbul

VICTORIA PEAK

POK FU LAM

East Asian porcupine

Porcupines have been sighted in some surprising areas. One was even seen taking a walk in the city centre!

Masked laughingthrush

The **masked palm civet** can be spotted eating fruit in the lush trees of the city's urban parks.

Tokay gecko

Growing up to 40cm long, the **tokay gecko** is the second largest gecko in the world.

Masked palm civet

Yellow-crested cockatoo

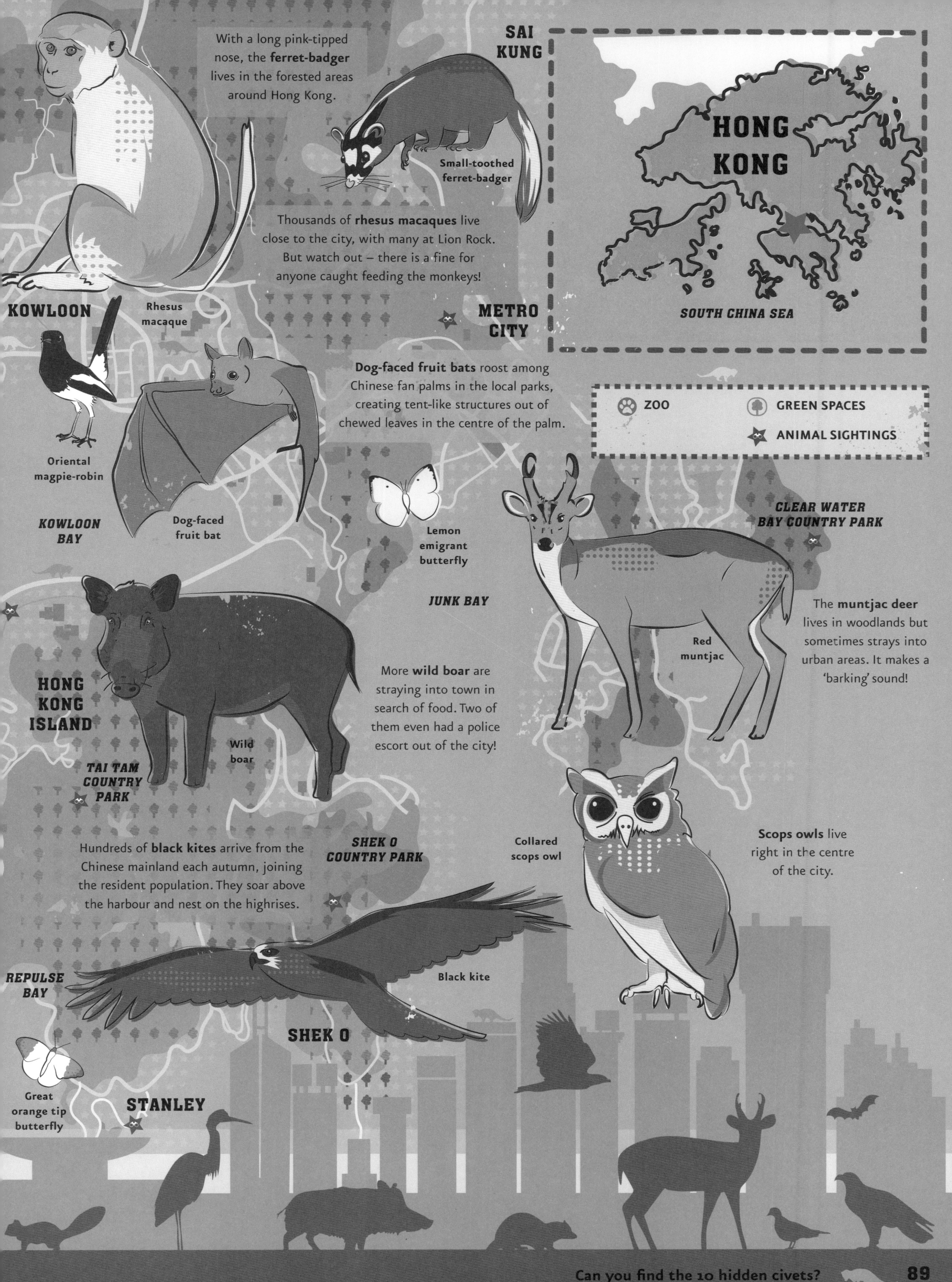
With a long pink-tipped nose, the **ferret-badger** lives in the forested areas around Hong Kong.
SAI KUNG
HONG KONG
Small-toothed ferret-badger
Thousands of **rhesus macaques** live close to the city, with many at Lion Rock. But watch out – there is a fine for anyone caught feeding the monkeys!
KOWLOON
Rhesus macaque
METRO CITY
SOUTH CHINA SEA
Dog-faced fruit bats roost among Chinese fan palms in the local parks, creating tent-like structures out of chewed leaves in the centre of the palm.
ZOO
GREEN SPACES
ANIMAL SIGHTINGS
Oriental magpie-robin
KOWLOON BAY
Dog-faced fruit bat
Lemon emigrant butterfly
CLEAR WATER BAY COUNTRY PARK
JUNK BAY
The **muntjac deer** lives in woodlands but sometimes strays into urban areas. It makes a 'barking' sound!
Red muntjac
More **wild boar** are straying into town in search of food. Two of them even had a police escort out of the city!
HONG KONG ISLAND
Wild boar
TAI TAM COUNTRY PARK
Hundreds of **black kites** arrive from the Chinese mainland each autumn, joining the resident population. They soar above the harbour and nest on the highrises.
SHEK O COUNTRY PARK
Collared scops owl
Scops owls live right in the centre of the city.
Black kite
REPULSE BAY
SHEK O
Great orange tip butterfly
STANLEY
Can you find the 10 hidden civets?

SHANGHAI

Shanghai is one of the biggest, most developed cities in the world. At its heart is the Bund, a historic centre of old buildings and pretty gardens, but opposite are the high-tech skyscrapers of the Pudong district. As in many Chinese cities, pollution is a problem, and the Yangtze River has particularly suffered. However, efforts are being made to protect wildlife, which hangs on in the small oases of green that pepper this urban jungle.

The biggest badger in the world, the **hog badger** has a piglike snout. It is occasionally seen on the fringes of the city.

WENZAOBANG RIVER

Black-crowned night heron

Red-eared pond slider

See **black-crowned night herons** right in the heart of the city in the Bund gardens and parks.

JIADING

There are lots of **frogs** in the waterways of the city. They are best seen and heard in the evenings.

Eastern golden frog

Chinese water deer

PUTUO

Chinese blackbird

PEOPLE'S PARK

CHANGFENG PARK

FUXING PARK

Raccoon dog

Asiatic toad

XUJIAHUI PARK

XUHUI

A group of wild **raccoon dogs** has set up home in the grounds of Shanghai Zoo, coming out after hours.

Field frog

SHANGHAI BOTANICAL GARDEN

The **Siberian weasel** is best known for one thing – catching rats. In fact, its Chinese name, huang shu lang, literally means 'yellow rat wolf'.

ANIMAL STORIES

'VAMPIRE' DEER

Chinese water deer are a small species, native to the lowlands and rivers of China. They do not have antlers but have downward-pointing tusks instead, which has led to their nickname, 'vampire deer'! Once widespread, the deer have been left close to extinction by overhunting and habitat loss.

The deer were last officially recorded in Shanghai in 1890, but a reintroduction programme started in 2006 is set to save them. A group of deer were released into the wild at the Nanhui Wildlife Sanctuary and the more urban Binjiang Forest Park, with plans to bring them to more parks. So this shy creature may still have a future in Shanghai.

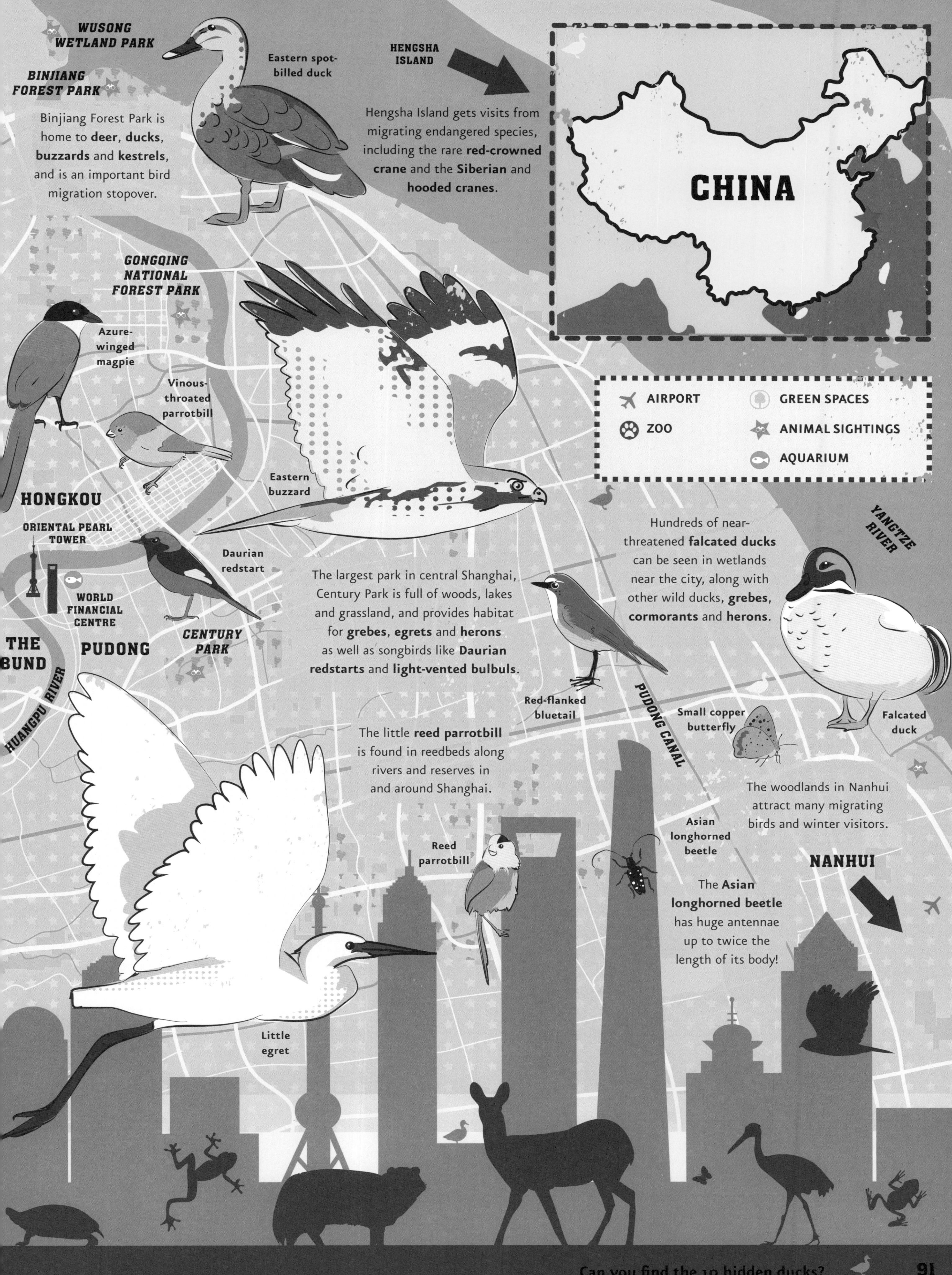
WUSONG WETLAND PARK
BINJIANG FOREST PARK
Binjiang Forest Park is home to **deer**, **ducks**, **buzzards** and **kestrels**, and is an important bird migration stopover.
Eastern spot-billed duck
HENGSHA ISLAND
Hengsha Island gets visits from migrating endangered species, including the rare **red-crowned crane** and the **Siberian** and **hooded cranes**.
CHINA
GONGQING NATIONAL FOREST PARK
Azure-winged magpie
Vinous-throated parrotbill
AIRPORT
GREEN SPACES
ZOO
ANIMAL SIGHTINGS
AQUARIUM
Eastern buzzard
HONGKOU
ORIENTAL PEARL TOWER
Daurian redstart
WORLD FINANCIAL CENTRE
THE BUND
PUDONG
CENTURY PARK
HUANGPU RIVER
YANGTZE RIVER
Hundreds of near-threatened **falcated ducks** can be seen in wetlands near the city, along with other wild ducks, **grebes**, **cormorants** and **herons**.
The largest park in central Shanghai, Century Park is full of woods, lakes and grassland, and provides habitat for **grebes**, **egrets** and **herons** as well as songbirds like **Daurian redstarts** and **light-vented bulbuls**.
Red-flanked bluetail
PUDONG CANAL
Small copper butterfly
Falcated duck
The little **reed parrotbill** is found in reedbeds along rivers and reserves in and around Shanghai.
The woodlands in Nanhui attract many migrating birds and winter visitors.
Asian longhorned beetle
Reed parrotbill
NANHUI
The **Asian longhorned beetle** has huge antennae up to twice the length of its body!
Little egret
Can you find the 10 hidden ducks?

SINGAPORE
This island city-state is a tropical paradise, where cutting-edge technology meets ancient rainforests. Although Singapore is one of the fastest-growing cities on the planet, more than 10 per cent of its area is given over to parks and reserves, including the Gardens by the Bay, a space dominated by 'supertrees' – tall man-made structures bursting with plants. What's more, this wild city hosts some of the world's most endangered creatures.
Sunda colugo
The endangered slow loris has special glands on its elbows which it licks to give it a toxic bite.
Sunda slow loris
Masters of camouflage, colugos, or flying lemurs, glide from tree to tree on wing-like membranes that stretch from their neck to their ankles.
Harlequin rasbora
Greater racket-tailed drongo
CENTRAL CATCHMENT NATURE RESERVE
BUKIT TIMAH NATURE RESERVE
Critically-endangered pangolins are illegally hunted for their meat, skin and scales. There are about 100 of them in reserves across Singapore.
Sunda pangolin
Plantain squirrel
Urban macaques try to steal food, which can lead to conflict with humans. The best way to help is to leave them alone and use special 'monkey-proof' bins.
CHINESE GARDEN
Long-tailed macaque
The plantain squirrel, with its red belly, is seen throughout the city, along with the slender squirrel, which has a grey belly.
JURONG BIRD PARK
BOON LAY
Common Mormon butterfly
Reticulated python
BOTANIC GARDENS
The most common snake in Singapore is the reticulated python, which grows up to 10m long and squeezes its prey to death. Pythons live in drains and have even been found in swimming pools!
Common tree shrew
Also known as the toddy cat, the civet lives in forests and urban areas, such as gardens and attics.
Common rose butterfly
Common palm civet
KENT RIDGE PARK
PEARL'S HILL CITY PARK
MOUNT FABER PARK
JURONG ISLAND
White-tailed eagle
SENTOSA

The introduced **banded bullfrog** sounds like a cow when it croaks!

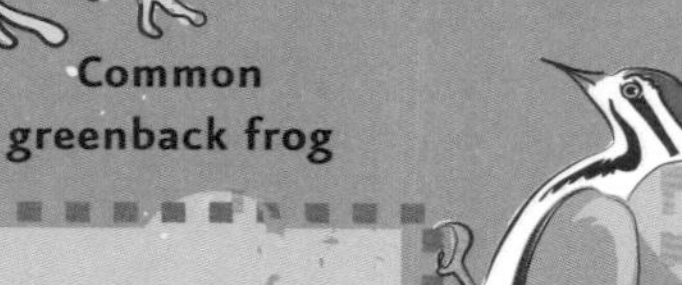

There are over 25 species of **frogs** and **toads** in Singapore.

Common greenback frog

AMAZING SPACES

Banded leaf monkey

Grey-headed fish eagle

Crimson sunbird

Lesser mouse-deer

Sunda scops owl

CENTRAL CATCHMENT RESERVE

The biggest reserve in Singapore, spanning rainforest and reservoirs, this green space is home to many animals, including the endangered slow loris, the banded leaf monkey and the rare flying squirrel.

SERANGOON ISLAND

Oriental white-eye

Cave nectar bats live in an underpass near the city centre. They are among 26 bat species in Singapore.

AIRPORT

ZOO

GREEN SPACES

ANIMAL SIGHTINGS

AQUARIUM

Common birdwing butterfly

TAMPINES

Smooth-coated otter

Red junglefowl

Cave nectar bat

BEDOK RESERVOIR

The **red junglefowl** is the wild ancestor of domestic chickens.

Straw-headed bulbul

EAST COAST PARK

Javan myna

DOWNTOWN

Green crested lizard

MBFC TOWER 3

GARDENS BY THE BAY

There are fewer than 2,000 **straw-headed bulbuls** in the wild but there are still some in Singapore.

Oriental pied hornbill

The **oriental pied hornbill** has been brought back to Singapore through the use of nest boxes and feeding stations. There are now over 100 birds in the area.

ANIMAL STORIES

OTTERLY AMAZING

Otters have made a comeback across Singapore, and one family is a popular attraction at the Bishan-Ang Mo Kio Park in the city's centre. Nicknamed the 'Bishan 10', they have become wildlife celebrities, featured in documentaries and constantly photographed. You can even hear the family's high-pitched squeaks as they talk to each other.

Incredibly, in 2015 otters were suspected of eating around £45,000 worth of ornamental koi fish from a hotel and a garden pond!

Can you find the 10 hidden otters?

TOKYO

The Tokyo area is the most populated urban space on the planet. Located at the head of Tokyo Bay, this vast Japanese city is a concrete jungle of highrises and bright lights, famous for its electronics industry. Despite this, varied wildlife can be found in the city's green pockets and waterways. Mount Takao in the western suburbs has flying squirrels, badgers and occasionally red-bottomed Japanese macaque monkeys!

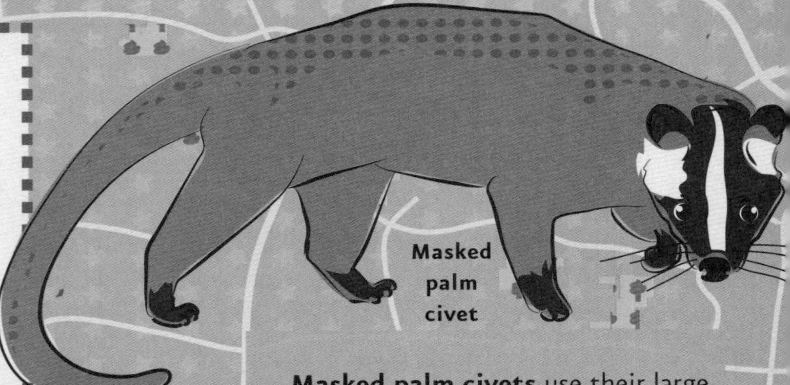

Masked palm civet

Masked palm civets use their large tails for balance as they climb the city's trees and power cables.

SHINJUKU

Japanese grass lizard

SHINJUKU GYOEN NATIONAL GARDEN

YOYOGI PARK

MEIJI SHRINE

The **softshell turtle** has a piglike snout.

Chinese softshell turtle

SETAGAYA

Japanese rat snake

Raccoon dog

Japanese white-eye

The **Japanese white-eye** loves to sip nectar from Japan's famous cherry blossom trees, which bloom in April.

KOMAZAWA OLYMPIC PARK

RINSHI NO MORI PARK

Japanese rat snakes grow up to 2m long and are often found in houses, chasing rats and mice. In fact, some Japanese people consider them a guardian of their home!

The **Japanese house bat** can be found roosting in attics or under bridges.

Japanese house bat

ANIMAL STORIES

TRICKY TANUKI

There are thought to be up to 1,000 raccoon dogs, or tanuki, in the Tokyo area. These nocturnal animals are about the size of a fox, but with distinctive eye markings like those of a raccoon.

The tanuki have a special place in Japanese culture. Legend has it they are mischievous shape-shifters that can take on a human form in order to play tricks on people. However, nowadays they are viewed as cheerful and loveable, and are thought to bring luck. People even have statues of them outside their place of work!

Japanese common toad

Snapping turtle

Schlegel's Japanese gecko

Large, aggressive **snapping turtles** have invaded Tokyo's waterways. They are thought to have bred from escaped or released pets.

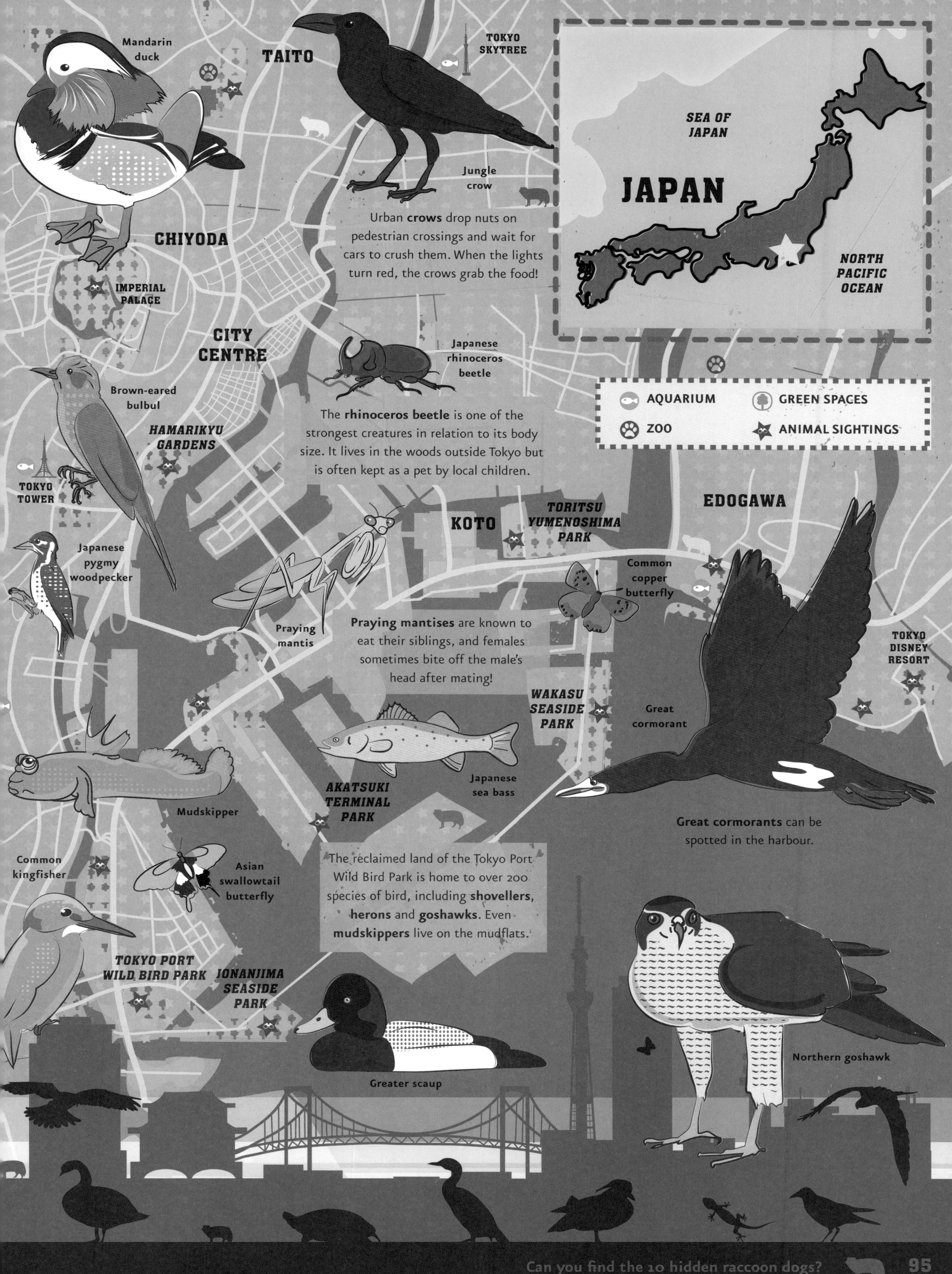

Mandarin duck
TAITO
TOKYO SKYTREE
SEA OF JAPAN
JAPAN
NORTH PACIFIC OCEAN
Jungle crow
Urban **crows** drop nuts on pedestrian crossings and wait for cars to crush them. When the lights turn red, the crows grab the food!
CHIYODA
IMPERIAL PALACE
CITY CENTRE
Japanese rhinoceros beetle
Brown-eared bulbul
AQUARIUM
GREEN SPACES
ZOO
ANIMAL SIGHTINGS
HAMARIKYU GARDENS
The **rhinoceros beetle** is one of the strongest creatures in relation to its body size. It lives in the woods outside Tokyo but is often kept as a pet by local children.
TOKYO TOWER
EDOGAWA
KOTO
TORITSU YUMENOSHIMA PARK
Japanese pygmy woodpecker
Common copper butterfly
Praying mantis
Praying mantises are known to eat their siblings, and females sometimes bite off the male's head after mating!
TOKYO DISNEY RESORT
WAKASU SEASIDE PARK
Great cormorant
Japanese sea bass
Mudskipper
AKATSUKI TERMINAL PARK
Great cormorants can be spotted in the harbour.
Common kingfisher
Asian swallowtail butterfly
The reclaimed land of the Tokyo Port Wild Bird Park is home to over 200 species of bird, including **shovellers**, **herons** and **goshawks**. Even **mudskippers** live on the mudflats.
TOKYO PORT WILD BIRD PARK
JONANJIMA SEASIDE PARK
Greater scaup
Northern goshawk
Can you find the 10 hidden raccoon dogs?

OCEANIA

Oceania is the name for the thousands of islands across the Pacific Ocean from America to Asia. Some, such as New Zealand, have only been inhabited in the last 700 years. Since then, human impact and invasive animal species have had a dramatic impact on the region's widlife. However, efforts are underway to halt this change and help native species make a comeback.

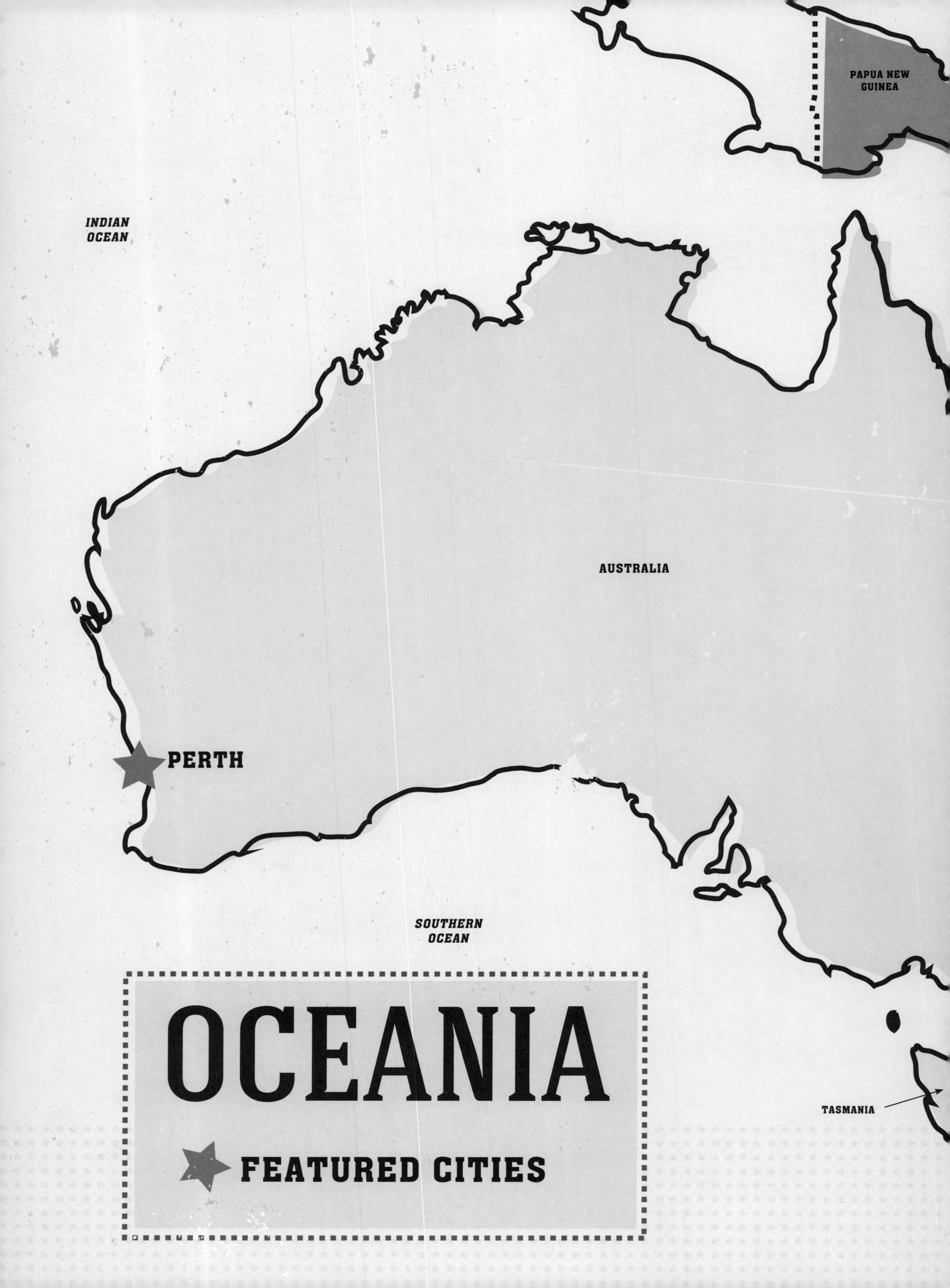
PAPUA NEW GUINEA
INDIAN OCEAN
AUSTRALIA
PERTH
SOUTHERN OCEAN
TASMANIA
OCEANIA
FEATURED CITIES

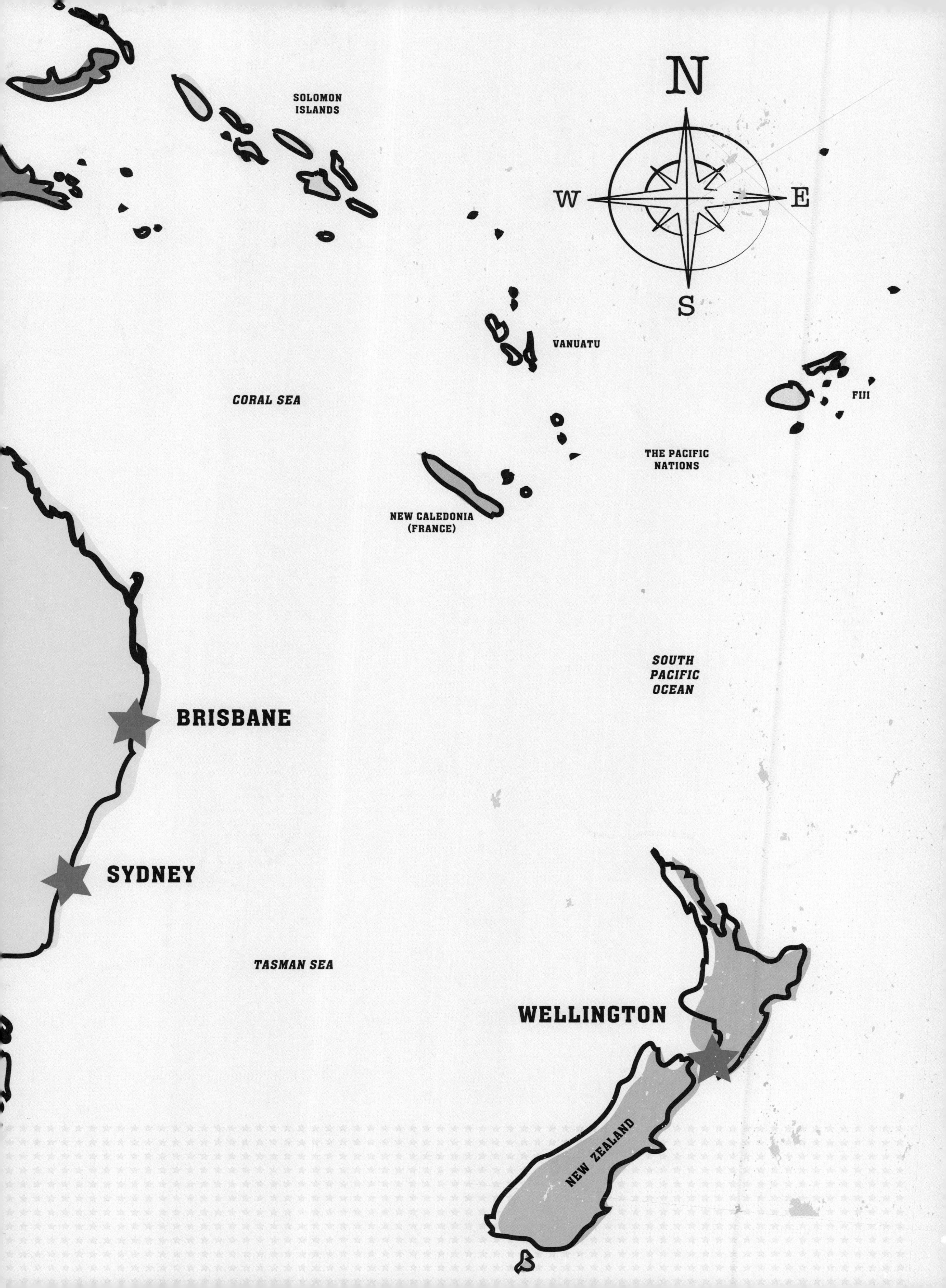
N
W
E
S
SOLOMON ISLANDS
VANUATU
CORAL SEA
FIJI
THE PACIFIC NATIONS
NEW CALEDONIA (FRANCE)
SOUTH PACIFIC OCEAN
BRISBANE
SYDNEY
TASMAN SEA
WELLINGTON
NEW ZEALAND

PERTH

Lapped by the warm waters of the Indian Ocean, the capital of Western Australia is a great place for spotting marine life, marsupials and fascinating reptiles. Beautiful sandy beaches fringe the coastline and the Swan River cuts through the city, bringing birdlife right into the heart of downtown. When Perth was founded, it was called the Swan River Colony because of all the black swans that lived on the riverbanks.

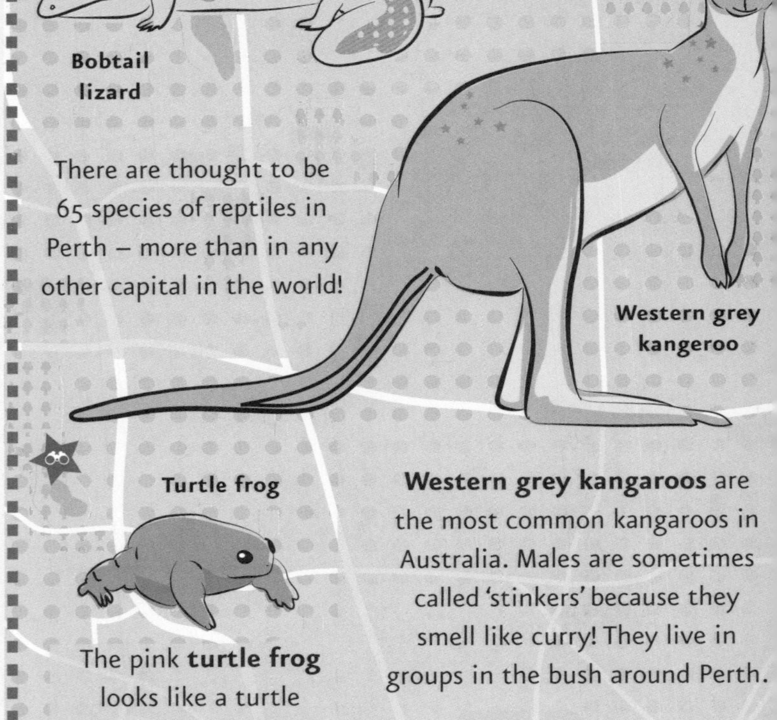

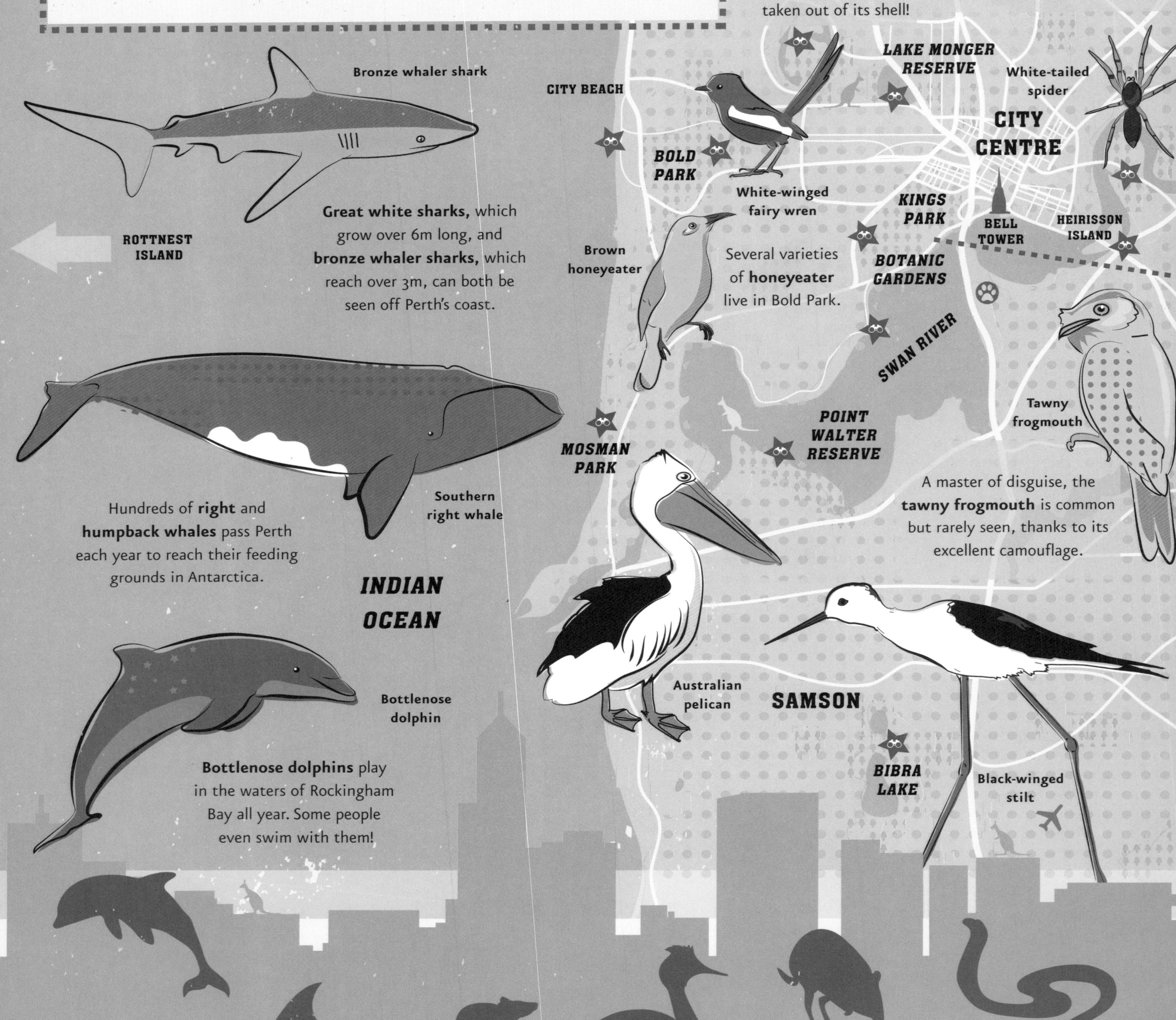

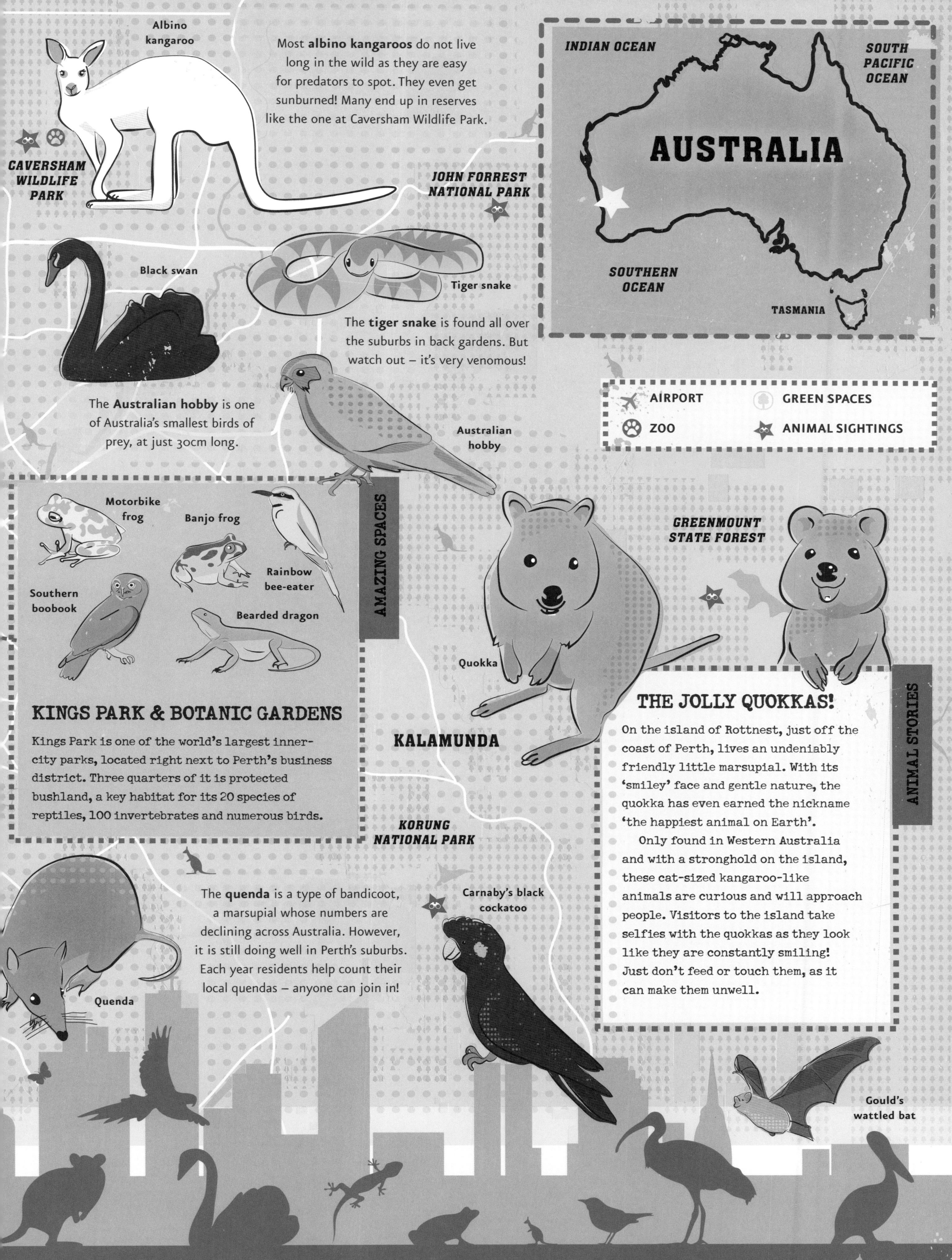

KINGS PARK & BOTANIC GARDENS

Kings Park is one of the world's largest inner-city parks, located right next to Perth's business district. Three quarters of it is protected bushland, a key habitat for its 20 species of reptiles, 100 invertebrates and numerous birds.

THE JOLLY QUOKKAS!

On the island of Rottnest, just off the coast of Perth, lives an undeniably friendly little marsupial. With its 'smiley' face and gentle nature, the quokka has even earned the nickname 'the happiest animal on Earth'.

Only found in Western Australia and with a stronghold on the island, these cat-sized kangaroo-like animals are curious and will approach people. Visitors to the island take selfies with the quokkas as they look like they are constantly smiling! Just don't feed or touch them, as it can make them unwell.

Can you find the 10 hidden kangaroos?

BRISBANE

The capital of Queensland is a great place to enjoy the outdoor life, on the banks of the winding River Brisbane, among the surrounding hills or on the neighbouring Sunshine Coast. The city has more species of plant, animal and insect than any other capital in Australia! Brisbane's bushland neighbours include wallabies, kangaroos and endangered koalas, and the city has a number of schemes to help protect vulnerable wildlife and their habitats.

Brisbane has around 20 permanent roosts of **flying foxes**, which hang from trees in the north of the city. In some seasons you can see more than 50,000 of them in one place!

Grey-headed flying fox

HENDRA

Huntsman spider

BRISBANE RIVER

Sulphur-crested cockatoo

Bush stone-curlew

CITY CENTRE

Huntsman spiders, which are 15cm wide, sometimes venture into homes and offices.

Watch out for **wallabies** on Mt Coot-tha, the highest peak in Brisbane at 287m.

MT COOT-THA

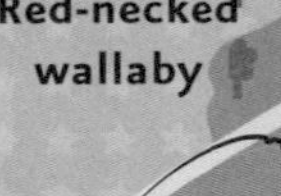

BRISBANE WHEEL

MINNIPPI PARKLANDS

Asian house gecko

Since arriving in Brisbane in the 1980s, **Asian house geckos** have spread across urban Australia.

Wild brush turkey

The **Australian white ibis** is sometimes called the 'tip turkey', because it is known for eating rubbish!

Koala

Australian white ibis

With their cuddly looks and lazy lifestyle, **koalas** are one of Australia's best-loved animals. Look for them at Point Halloran Conservation Reserve or see them snoozing in the trees at the Lone Pine Koala Santuary.

MOUNT GRAVATT

LONE PINE KOALA SANCTUARY

ROCKS RIVERSIDE PARK

Southern laughing tree frog

Squirrel glider

Brushtail possum

Brown goshawk

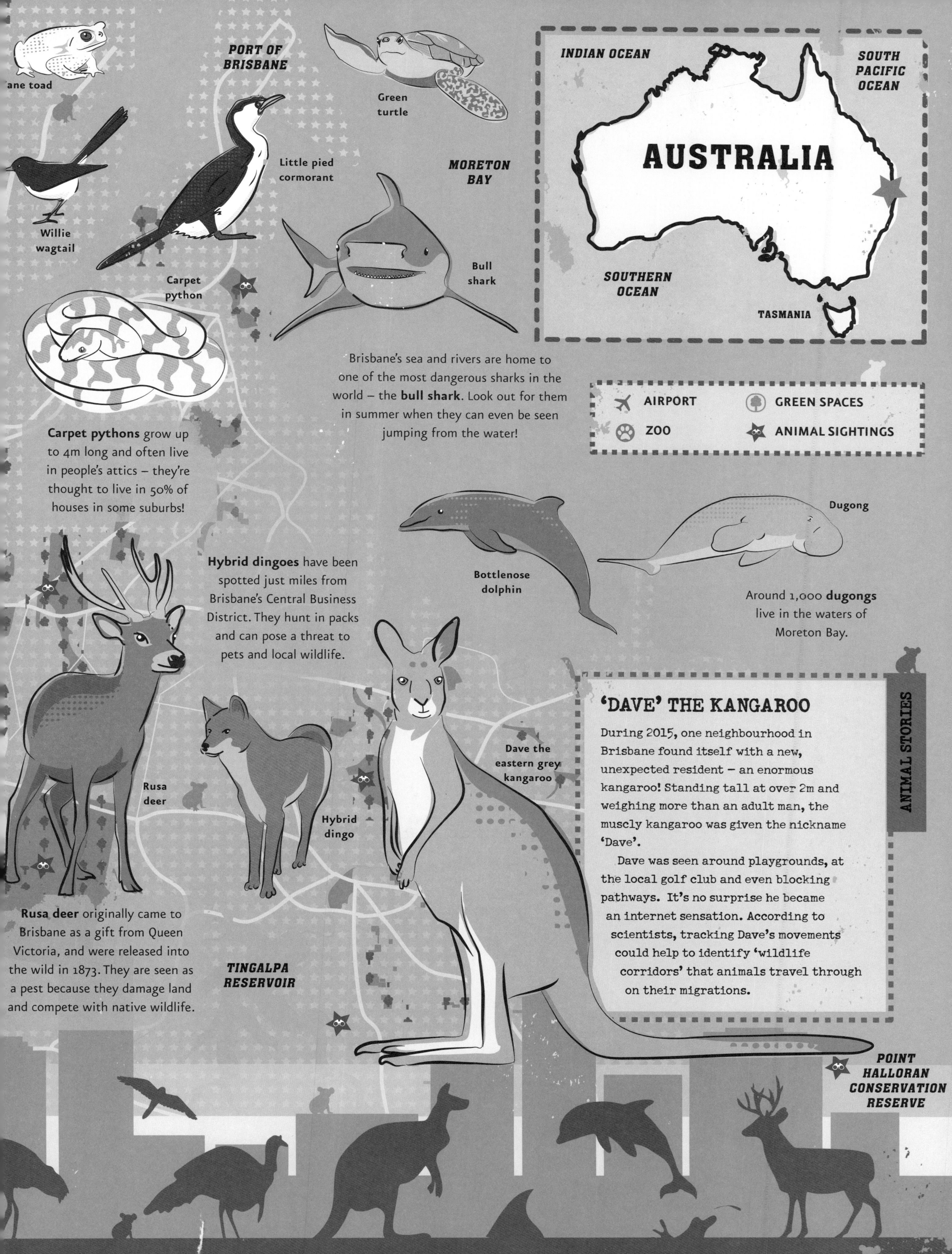

Carpet pythons grow up to 4m long and often live in people's attics – they're thought to live in 50% of houses in some suburbs!

Brisbane's sea and rivers are home to one of the most dangerous sharks in the world – the **bull shark**. Look out for them in summer when they can even be seen jumping from the water!

Hybrid dingoes have been spotted just miles from Brisbane's Central Business District. They hunt in packs and can pose a threat to pets and local wildlife.

Around 1,000 **dugongs** live in the waters of Moreton Bay.

Rusa deer originally came to Brisbane as a gift from Queen Victoria, and were released into the wild in 1873. They are seen as a pest because they damage land and compete with native wildlife.

'DAVE' THE KANGAROO

During 2015, one neighbourhood in Brisbane found itself with a new, unexpected resident – an enormous kangaroo! Standing tall at over 2m and weighing more than an adult man, the muscly kangaroo was given the nickname 'Dave'.

Dave was seen around playgrounds, at the local golf club and even blocking pathways. It's no surprise he became an internet sensation. According to scientists, tracking Dave's movements could help to identify 'wildlife corridors' that animals travel through on their migrations.

Can you find the 10 hidden koalas?

SYDNEY

Sydney is the largest, oldest and busiest city in Australia. It is famous for its Opera House, Harbour Bridge and surfing beaches. Surrounded by national park, the city offers a fantastic sample of urban wildlife, with exotic birds, mammals, frogs, spiders and 40 species of reptiles to be glimpsed across town. Sydney also sits on the world's largest natural harbour, which brings in marine life, such as dolphins, whales and plenty of sharks!

Diamond python

Grey-headed flying fox

A large colony of **flying foxes** can be seen in the Botanic Gardens, most often at sunset. Despite their name, they are large, furry bats. They only eat fruit and pollen.

Eastern water dragon

See **Eastern water dragons** up close at the Chinese Garden.

Green and golden bell frog

SYDNEY OLYMPIC PARK

PROSPECT NATURE RESERVE

Sydney funnel-web spider

Several **green and golden bell frogs** were found on Sydney's Olympic Park during construction – so the tennis court planned for the site had to be moved elsewhere!

ROOKWOOD

The **Sydney funnel-web spider** has one of the most dangerous bites of any spider!

Kookaburra

AUBURN BOTANIC GARDENS

Common brushtail possum

The **common brushtail possum** has adapted to urban living after much of its habitat was destroyed. In fact, these large possums are commonly found inside roofs!

Eastern blue-tongued lizard

ANIMAL STORIES

LAUGH, KOOKABURRA!

The distinctive 'laugh' of the kookaburra is a well-known sound across Sydney. Every morning the birds call out from their treetop homes to mark their territory. This loud, cackle-like sound even gave them their name!

Kookaburras are large members of the kingfisher family. They eat small animals such as lizards and insects. Although kookaburras are found all over Sydney, they shot to wordwide fame in 2000 when 'Olly' the kookaburra became one of the mascots of the Sydney Olympics. The Australian men's national hockey team is also named after this loud but friendly bird!

HURSTVILLE

Meadow argus butterfly

Powerful owl

Look out for **powerful owls** roosting across the city, and listen for their 'woo-hoo' calls.

GEORGES RIVER NATIONAL PARK

Bar-tailed godwit

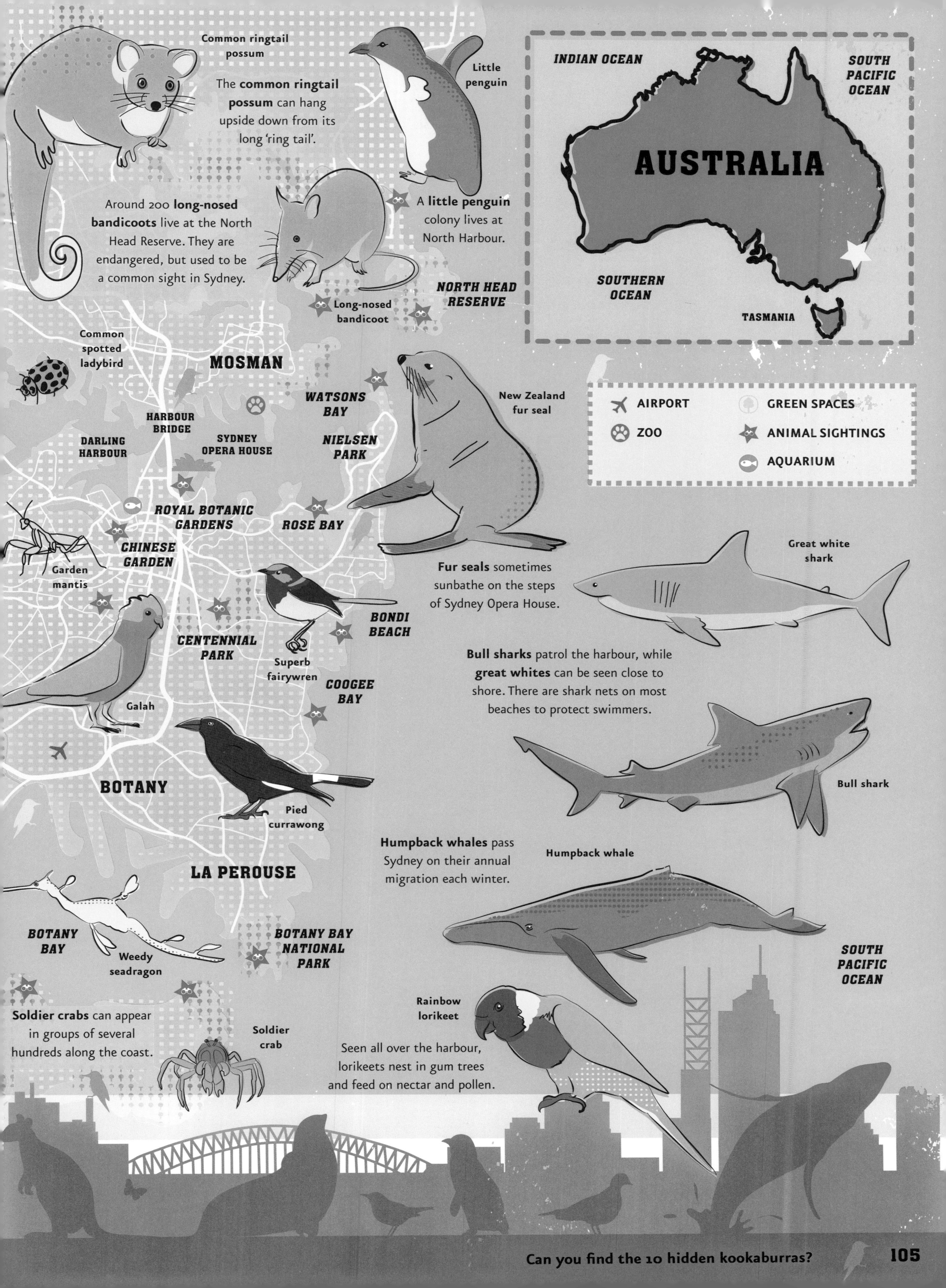
Common ringtail possum
The **common ringtail possum** can hang upside down from its long 'ring tail'.
Little penguin
A **little penguin** colony lives at North Harbour.
Around 200 **long-nosed bandicoots** live at the North Head Reserve. They are endangered, but used to be a common sight in Sydney.
Long-nosed bandicoot
NORTH HEAD RESERVE
INDIAN OCEAN
SOUTH PACIFIC OCEAN
AUSTRALIA
SOUTHERN OCEAN
TASMANIA
Common spotted ladybird
MOSMAN
WATSONS BAY
HARBOUR BRIDGE
DARLING HARBOUR
SYDNEY OPERA HOUSE
NIELSEN PARK
New Zealand fur seal
AIRPORT
ZOO
GREEN SPACES
ANIMAL SIGHTINGS
AQUARIUM
ROYAL BOTANIC GARDENS
ROSE BAY
CHINESE GARDEN
Garden mantis
Fur seals sometimes sunbathe on the steps of Sydney Opera House.
Great white shark
BONDI BEACH
CENTENNIAL PARK
Superb fairywren
COOGEE BAY
Galah
Bull sharks patrol the harbour, while **great whites** can be seen close to shore. There are shark nets on most beaches to protect swimmers.
BOTANY
Bull shark
Pied currawong
Humpback whales pass Sydney on their annual migration each winter.
Humpback whale
LA PEROUSE
BOTANY BAY
Weedy seadragon
BOTANY BAY NATIONAL PARK
SOUTH PACIFIC OCEAN
Rainbow lorikeet
Soldier crabs can appear in groups of several hundreds along the coast.
Soldier crab
Seen all over the harbour, lorikeets nest in gum trees and feed on nectar and pollen.
Can you find the 10 hidden kookaburras?

WELLINGTON

The capital of New Zealand faces onto a stormy channel dividing the country's North and South Islands. Downtown, it is bursting with museums, galleries and restaurants, but only a hop out of the city is one of New Zealand's most ground-breaking nature reserves. Established to protect native species from introduced mammals, Zealandia Ecosanctuary is part of Wellington's aim to become the world's first predator-free capital.

ZEALANDIA ECOSANCTUARY

Zealandia is a unique sanctuary in the suburbs of Wellington, completely surrounded by a predator-proof fence. The sanctuary plans to restore the ecosytem to the way it was before humans arrived in AD 1300, by reintroducing native plants and animals, and by removing species introduced by humans.

BACK FROM THE BRINK

Like many of New Zealand's native birds, the kaka's numbers dwindled through the nineteenth century as the parrot's habitat was destroyed and it was preyed on by introduced mammals. It had been extinct in Wellington for nearly a century when six captive birds were released into the wild in 2002.

Today there are more than 300 kaka in Wellington's parks and gardens! The inquisitive birds can damage trees and buildings with their big beaks and are very noisy – but their return has been welcomed by residents.

Can you find the 10 hidden kaka?

INDEX